My Anchor Holds Within the Veil

Bipolar Disorder and God's Providence

Micah T. Yarborough

&

Bobbi Jo H. Yarborough

My Anchor Holds Within the Veil

ISBN: 1984930842
ISBN-13: 978-1984930842

Book design by Peter Yue (peteryue.com)

For my sister Sarah, who told
me I should read more...
and look, I wrote a book.

1975 - 1991

When darkness veils
His lovely face,
I rest on His unchanging grace;
In every high and stormy gale,
My anchor holds
within the veil.

Edward Mote ca. 1834

CONTENTS

Thank you Ron Marrs for meeting and praying with me throughout the writing of this book. Your friendship has been an encouragement. Gentleness and humility are characteristics I continually need to cultivate; spending time with someone who consistently models these virtues has been most helpful to that end.

Coming Unmoored

It was a cold and foggy November morning; I had been out in the bay before dawn. In fact, for the past several days I had been making my way to this inlet in the Puget Sound before sunrise. On this particular morning I had just reeled in a chum salmon, but as I released it back into the harbor, the combination of the frigid water and the slimy fish caused my wedding ring to slip off into the shallow silt of the shoreline beneath me. I felt the ring slip away. Frantically, I combed through the tidewater at my feet. It was still fairly dark out and the tide was coming in quickly. I searched the murky water in vain but the ring was gone. Soaking wet I walked a quarter mile back to my parents' house where my wife, Bobbi, was waiting. I felt angry, anxious, and perhaps more than anything else, determined.

I remember very little of what transpired over the next four months, only glimpses of certain things here and there. Bobbi tells me that I returned to my parents' home and immediately left again to purchase the first of three metal detectors. When one failed to locate my ring, I insisted on purchasing another. The next memory I have, from the following day, is of seeing a shattered mirror outside our bedroom in our house. I know that I broke the mirror, but I have no memory of how or why.

After that, the only clear recollection I have is from later that same evening. I remember feeling as if I were waking from a dream. I was standing in a luxury furniture store talking to Bobbi on my cell phone. She was desperately trying to convince me that the $11,000 worth of bedroom furniture I had just purchased was an ill-conceived idea. I couldn't be dissuaded. Our full-length mirror was broken and needed to be replaced. Because she and I had been talking about purchasing new bedroom furniture anyway, from my point of view I was taking care of both problems. Eventually Bobbi got through to me that night and for the first time I realized that something was very, very wrong.

When I first slid Micah's wedding ring on his finger we could only imagine a bright future ahead. But as it slipped away that dim morning just three years later, it took so much with it: first, my husband's tenuous grasp on reality, later his hope.

When Micah returned after losing his ring I was obviously disappointed but I could see right away that any grief I might have felt would have to wait. "It's just a material possession," I reminded myself. He was angry and intent on finding the ring which was, of course, hopelessly lost in the Puget Sound. Nevertheless, he spent the entire day combing the beach whenever the tide went out and dredging the shallow areas as it came back in. At first, I pled with him and then later demanded that he come in from the pouring rain, but I was ignored. When he finally did come inside, he was sullen. I tried to comfort him, other family members tried to console him, finally everyone just left him alone.

The next day we needed to return to our home three hours away. We had hardly spoken to one another, and it was clear to our family that Micah needed to be given more space and time. We all felt he was overreacting, and everyone recognized how strangely he was behaving but we didn't understand why or what we should do about it.

He packed our things into the trunk of our car and waited at the wheel while I said goodbye to his parents, who were both appalled by his behavior. I noticed Micah's impatience as we drove away. When we reached the freeway, he began darting in and out of traffic, passing cars and far exceeding the speed limit. Soon he was honking the horn and swearing at other drivers. This behavior was extremely unusual for my husband who is typically a very cautious, easygoing driver. As we raced south along the I-5 corridor between Seattle and Portland, I begged him to slow down. He wove in and out of traffic, his eyes focused on the road as if I weren't even there.

I had always taken comfort in Micah's protection of me, but now, as buildings, cars, and signs whirred past, I barely recognized the wild-eyed stranger beside me. I became angry—at his ridiculous obsession with the lost ring, at how he had treated his family, at how selfish he was acting. I urged him to stop the car, even just to let me out. I thought my anger would provoke him, but he remained focused on the road and kept speeding ahead.

I felt like a hostage; I had never been more terrified. I wanted to call the police, but my cell phone was out of reach in my purse in the backseat, and I was too afraid to remove my seatbelt to retrieve it. I was even more afraid of his reaction. Would he come to his senses or, more likely it seemed, continue in a high-speed chase? I knew if I involved the police, he would face serious consequences, but I honestly feared that if I didn't, we would die or kill someone. This was a silent negotiation I would come to make many more times in the future—do I seek help for Micah, knowing the costs, or do we try to handle this on our own? I prayed for most of that drive home. When we miraculously parked at the curb outside of our house, I didn't know what to do next.

A few minutes later I collected myself and followed Micah, who had already gone into the house. I found him in our bedroom, rifling through his dresser drawers. Taking a deep breath, I asked him what was going on. In the space of a few minutes he was packing a bag, despite the fact that he had a fully packed bag still in the trunk of our car.

I panicked. I didn't want him behind the wheel of a car again. He was muttering to himself, slamming drawers, and saying something about how he needed to leave. I put my hand on his arm to get him to look at me, but he angrily swept it away. I asked him where he was going as he pushed past me and yelled something about how he couldn't stay and how I must not really love him if I didn't feel safe with him.

It was then that our mirror was shattered. I think he must have thrown something at it, or maybe just in its general direction. I felt dazed and helpless. I tried to figure out what to do. Again, I considered calling the police, or my family, or his family, but I honestly didn't know what I would tell them. That my husband was acting really strangely? That he had left suddenly and angrily and was probably driving dangerously? Given that little information, would the police be able to do anything? I didn't even know where he might have gone. What would my family or his family be able to do? I returned to prayer, this time for Micah's protection, for the protection of anyone else on the road, and for Micah to come to his senses and return home so things could go back to normal. But things wouldn't return to normal for a long time.

A few hours later, after I had called his phone numerous times, Micah finally called me. He simply said, "I saw that you called." He didn't sound angry or apologetic. When I asked where he was, he casually proceeded to tell me that he was just leaving a furniture store.

That was unexpected. I am a clinical psychologist, I was a student at the time but I already had some experience working with people whose behavior and thinking were occasionally affected by mental illness so I did what seemed appropriate, what I might do with a client in a similar situation. When I wanted to shout, "What the hell are you doing?!" I instead worked hard to maintain an emotionally flat tone of voice, matching his, and I asked him to tell me why he had been at a furniture store. In detail and at length and great speed, he described several pieces of furniture he had just purchased for our bedroom. When he explained that he knew how much I wanted new furniture, rather than confront him, I told him that I appreciated his consideration and reminded him of how much I enjoyed choosing pieces of furniture with him.

I could feel a sense of connection between us, although it was fragile. He went on to tell me how much I would like the furniture. When I wanted to say, "There is no way all of that will fit in our small bedroom," I instead complimented his taste and told him I was glad we had similar decorating sensibilities. When I felt him coming around to reason, I reminded him of our mutual agreement that we would not make large purchases (certainly not purchases totaling more than $10,000) without talking about it first. He defended himself by reminding me that minutes ago I had said he was thoughtful. I backed off but was encouraged that he was tracking our conversation.

I reminded him that we had recently bought a house, that we had just completed a costly repair of the water line, and that I had just returned to graduate school, so, financially speaking, it might not be the best time to refurnish our bedroom. I assured him that I looked forward to making our house a home together. For a moment, Micah could see that he had overstepped. He agreed to come home, and I asked him to put the salesperson on the line. I wondered what could possibly come next.

The Start of Things

One unseasonably warm December day when I was 14 my family and I were at the Washington coast watching my younger brother compete in a soccer tournament. A police officer arrived and notified my parents that my sister had been in an accident and that we needed to return home. My sixteen-year-old sister, who was on the high school drill team, had remained at home that weekend, to support the basketball team during the state playoff games. Another family offered to bring my brother home later and my parents and I left immediately.

My father drove directly to the home of a family

friend whose daughter had been staying at our house with my sister. Upon arrival, I waited in the car, anxious about what was unfolding. Not long after my parents entered the house, my dad came back out on the front porch. I nervously got out of the car and walked up the steps to him. With an artificially calm demeanor, my father said, "Son, your sister is dead. Someone murdered her today."

We would later learn that my sister had arrived on campus that morning an hour earlier than her drill teammates; she had written down the wrong start time in her day planner. There were only a few people running on the nearby track, but she had parked out of their view. Someone, possibly a transient stranger passing through the area, took advantage of her vulnerability and took her life. Though it remains under investigation, her case is still unsolved today.

When I heard my father's words, I couldn't take them in. I felt an immediate, overwhelming rush of intense anger, fear, and gut-wrenching sadness—but then, almost as suddenly as the emotions began, they ceased, and I felt nothing. I went inside the house and found the closest bathroom. My ears were ringing, and I felt as if my entire body was tingling. I locked the door and just stared at myself in the mirror. I didn't recognize the person staring back. He looked like me, but when I looked in his eyes, it was as if I wasn't there. I remember the haunting sound of my mother's sobbing, the sound of her heart breaking, a sound I will never forget.

For about six months I remained numb, robotically going about my daily routine of school and sports. Then, that summer, in many ways my life began to look like that of any other teenage boy. I began the ninth grade that fall, my final year in junior high. I did fine in my classes without any major difficulties. I played quarterback on the football team that season and performed as well as I generally always had. However, when football ended and I transitioned to basketball, I began to notice a change in myself.

I felt a heavy darkness, an emptiness. I was exhausted all the time even though I was getting enough sleep and was in great physical shape. Worse—and what starkly stood out to me at the time—was my abrupt and inexplicable inability to play basketball. I started the season well, but as I neared our first game, my body just didn't seem to work right. I couldn't shoot accurately and regularly missed the basket. Things that used to come naturally suddenly were tremendously challenging. I became angry and embarrassed, frustrated that I couldn't compete. Athletics had always been a defining part of my identity.

Around that time I started having significant sleep problems. Soon I couldn't focus, and my grades began slipping. Because I had been falling asleep in class, a teacher once asked me, rather bluntly, if I was on drugs. I strongly denied any drug use and left the classroom indignantly, failing to recognize her concern for me. Looking back now, it's easy to see how such a drastic and sudden change in a student, especially one in my circumstances, might lead someone to that conclusion. Everyone in the school district knew of my sister's death because it had happened on the school grounds and devastated the community. Surely concerned teachers were watching my brother and me. I couldn't give the teacher an explanation because, frankly, I had no idea what was happening to me and I lacked the ability to articulate how I was feeling and what I was going through. I just wanted to get back to my normal life, but I wouldn't experience any enduring sense of normalcy for the next 17 years.

Feeling unsure of what to do, my parents sent me to see a psychiatrist. I don't remember much about the visit except that I didn't feel very comfortable and I didn't like the guy. I believe he told my parents I was depressed and prescribed an antidepressant. It left me feeling even more tired and didn't seem to help at all. I remained empty and miserable, detached from everything around me, unable to enjoy anything.

My sleep problems were worsening. I often stayed up all night. Agitated, I would leave my house after my parents went to sleep and wander around the city alone seeking to escape the gnawing feeling of restlessness. I felt unsettled and unstable, like I could never calm down or relax. My grades continued to deteriorate and again that spring I struggled to compete, this time in baseball, my favorite sport. By the end of that summer, I had started drinking alcohol. This was uncharacteristic of me, but I was becoming someone else. I didn't care anymore. I quickly learned that drinking excessively temporarily attenuated my misery. I never talked to anyone about how I was feeling or what was going on inside me.

That fall I was to start high school but the thought of being on the same campus where my sister was murdered terrified me, so I enrolled in a private high school in another city. The change was both good and bad for me. The academic expectations and behavioral standards were much higher and the environment was much more structured than the public schools I had attended. I had always thrived in environments such as this, with ample supports. But the transition was hard because I only knew one person and I no longer possessed the charm and social skills I once had. I had lost the ability to make friends and lacked self-confidence. I started having paranoid thoughts for the first time that winter, but because I had also begun occasionally smoking pot, I assumed it was just part of that experience. The other people I smoked pot with joked about feeling paranoid, but their experiences were always kind of humorous; my thoughts grew dark and strange even when I was not high. I never told anyone about these thoughts.

While I spent time with friends, I generally preferred solitude. I stayed up late reading or just crying without really understanding why. I hated the deep feeling of loneliness I felt, but I discovered that sex temporarily made me feel better. Soon I had sex as often as I possibly could, which was generally all

I wanted from the girls I slept with. I was cold and uncaring and treated them all poorly. They were a means to an end for me. Having grown up in the church, I knew the Bible was clear that sex was meant to be enjoyed within marriage, but I didn't care. I only cared about getting my needs met. Over time I became increasingly inwardly focused and selfish. I started doing things that were wrong, like petty theft and vandalism, just because they were wrong. I was also becoming a habitual and very skilled liar.

Over the course of the next summer, I continued to morph into a different person. My mood didn't improve; instead, I became angrier, more irritable, and a good deal more reckless. Even though it numbed me, I didn't really like to drink and usually felt terrible afterwards; getting high made me feel kind of stupid and tired. Nevertheless, I was committed to a path of self-destruction. I started drinking more frequently, sometimes to great excess. I played junior legion baseball that summer, and one night I drank way too much. When my ride to the game showed up early the next morning, I was still intoxicated but made efforts to hide it. It was an hour ride to the field and when the game began, I stood at shortstop in the first inning, realizing that I was still not yet fully sober.

I don't remember the game or how I played, but as the game began, I thought, "What are you doing? This isn't like you, I can't believe you did this." Still, I ignored the clear warning that I was making terrible decisions. I truly didn't care about anything. I felt emotionally out of control and imbalanced almost all the time. My instability was evident when, near the end of the season, I completely lost control and told off my coaches. I quit the team and made fool of myself in the process. I had always been prone to losing my temper, but until then I could also be very gentle and kind. Over that summer and fall any compassion or mercy I had was replaced with cold cynicism. I was surly.

I stopped putting effort into school and continued to withdraw socially. I stopped thinking about the future and only thought of the present, how miserable I felt, and how justified I was in doing whatever I wanted that would make me feel better. I treated everyone terribly—my parents, my brother, friends, girlfriends, and even my teachers. I began missing more school and I knew I was failing a few classes. Knowing public school would be easier, I made up my mind that I would leave the prep school I had been attending and resume at my local high school following the Christmas holiday break.

Over that holiday break my behavior became increasingly erratic. I even blew up at my mother at a holiday meal in my grandparents' home. When it came time to return to school I basically never went. I couldn't sit still and couldn't endure sitting through even one period. Within just a few weeks, I was failing all of my classes. I was getting little to no sleep at night so someone suggested to my mother that I take melatonin. I was so sleep deprived that I actually wet the bed when I finally slept that night. Later, when my girlfriend made light of it, I lost my composure and threw something at her that could have really injured her.

Storming out of the house, I went for a drive. I ended up in an area where there was a big bowl-shaped depression with a four-way stop at the bottom and straightaways leading up to it in each direction. I don't know how long I did this, but I drove back and forth as fast as I possibly could through that bowl. It felt so good to drive that fast and to dip down then rise up again. I did it over and over at high speeds, wishing it would never stop. Eventually I headed home where an officer was waiting for me because my parents had called the police out of concern. I was issued a warning and the police officer left.

In the aftermath of that event I got the idea that I needed to go back to the coastal town where I had been when my sister was killed. I think I believed that by going back I could get back to the life I had before she died. My mother, my girlfriend, and I went to stay in the same hotel our family had stayed that infamous weekend. It rained most of the time we were there and a very large puddle had formed in the grass between our door and the nearby sand dunes. I went out there in the cold rain, fully clothed, running and sliding headfirst into that large puddle. I alternated screaming and yelling and crying. Later, I drove my compact car onto the sand and went all along the beach, swerving in and out of the water as the waves crashed. Once I got back out onto the street, the car died and had to be taken to a repair shop.

At one point that weekend I decided I would try to end my life, so I coerced my girlfriend into stealing some beer for me at a convenience store. I had stolen medication from my mother and I got drunk and took it. I filled up a large bath and wondered if I could pass out deep enough to slip into the water and drown.

As I began to feel like I was fading out, I started trying to go down into the water and hold my breath, hoping I would lose consciousness while I was under, but I was never able to pass out. Eventually I gave up and stumbled out of the bathroom, completely wasted. When the weekend was over I made the two-and-a-half-hour drive home in the pouring rain at dangerously high speeds with my girlfriend in the car. I was driving completely out of control on the freeway, but it felt exhilarating.

My mother observed much of what happened that weekend and I told her about trying to kill myself. My parents decided I needed help—and I knew it, too—so I agreed to a psychiatric evaluation. It was recommended that I go into inpatient treatment for mental health and substance use problems. I was very confused at that time, and I don't think I was capable of giving my assent; I don't think I was fully aware that I would be locked in and unable to leave. When I arrived at the facility, I think I slept for two days and the staff mostly left me alone. Then it began to dawn on me that I was stuck there. My restless energy was gone and I felt angry and tired. And very alone.

I was given an orientation to the facility and

told what accomplishments I had to make to be able to leave. It was a dual-treatment facility, which meant you could receive treatment for both mental illnesses and substance use problems, but most of the focus was on the latter. I was told that most of my problems resulted from substance use but I disagreed. I hadn't been using drugs for very long or nearly as frequently or as heavily as many people I knew. I only recreationally dabbled in pot, which I had already lost interest in. In fact, I had no interest in any drugs or even alcohol and I wasn't physiologically or psychologically addicted to either. My life was a mess and I was locked in a facility. I didn't want anything more of what had gotten me there. Nevertheless, I was repeatedly told that I was in denial and that I had to accept my problem. The thing was, I didn't have a problem admitting I was using drugs and alcohol—but I didn't think drugs and alcohol were *the* problem.

Eventually, after considerable pressure, I admitted to being an alcoholic and an addict but I felt like a fraud. I felt a tension between pressure to take on this addict identity and my understanding (from their teaching) of what it meant to be an addict or alcoholic. I didn't think it fit, but I realized that I would have to stay longer if I didn't progress through the program. As I continued this day-in, day-out re-education I began to believe it. I began to think that maybe all the problems I had *were* completely due to drugs and alcohol. How else could I have ended up in a place like that? No one ever talked to me about having mental health problems. My parents were in full agreement that my problems were due to alcohol and drugs, so I felt pressure from them to adopt this new identity as well.

I hated that facility. I hated being locked in and told where to go and what to do. It provoked my rebellious spirit, but I knew that resisting would only lengthen my stay. I regularly had nightmares that the person who killed my sister (or some other evil person) would break into the facility to kill me and I had no escape because I was confined. I woke up many nights in a cold sweat. The whole experience left me convinced that I would never go to a place like that again. Years later, when I was an adult and very mentally ill and in need of hospitalization, I adamantly refused to go because I couldn't bear the thought of being imprisoned again.

Eventually, I graduated from the program and was allowed to go home. My parents picked me up and the hour-long car ride home was spent in complete silence. I left that place with no skills to cope with mental illness, nor was I receiving any mental health treatment. The counselors at the facility convinced me that any drugs—even psychiatric drugs—were bad for me. As a result, I went without treatment of any kind until my junior year of college. Yet when I look back on the events that led to that inpatient stay, it's clear to me now that I had my first manic episode. I did not recognize what had happened as mania at the time, nor did my parents. I doubt even the people that were providing my care in the inpatient facility recognized it, if they did it was never mentioned. Only later, as an adult, after I was reflecting on another manic episode, did I make the connection that I had had the same impulsive, reckless behaviors, the same feelings of euphoria during the months leading up to residential treatment.

The following summer my health began to improve. After apologizing to my baseball coaches, I was allowed to play on the American Legion senior team. For the most part I enjoyed it and played well, but my confidence was low and I had trouble relaxing on the field. The most important thing to me at that point was figuring out how I would graduate on time from high school. That fall I started taking community college courses. I did much better in the college setting because I didn't have to spend as many hours in a classroom and most of my grades depended on tests. Despite an episode of what I would later come to understand was depression, my grades improved.

While I was in inpatient treatment, I decided if I stopped sleeping with my girlfriend and lying all the time, God would be pleased with me. However, when I got out, I went right back to the same habits. I had no desire to change my ways and as my life seemed to be coming back together, I didn't think I needed God's help anymore.

The summer after I graduated from high school, I played summer baseball one last time and it felt very much like my early years of playing in the summer before my sister was killed. I had fun and found pleasure in competing. It was a relief to be able to relax. My plan was to go to community college for another year then transfer to a four-year college, but I had no idea that God was about to intervene in my life in an unexpected way.

At the end of the summer, I got a call from the local director of Young Life (a Christian youth group) who also was a family friend. He said a baseball coach at a small Christian college in Oregon asked if he knew of any good baseball players in the area who were Christians. My friend gave the coach my name and he wanted to watch me play. From a very young age I had wanted to participate in college-level athletics, but I had come to accept that much of my talent had been lost. I thought this was a consequence of poor decisions I had been making, and though that was some of it, I would later learn that some of those losses, as well as some of those decisions, were also the result of emerging mental illness.

I played very well that summer and I was just happy to be competing again. The thought of being able to play baseball for a few more years was enticing, but I was not thrilled at the idea of going to a small Christian college. While I thought of myself as a Christian, I acted nothing like one and I dearly loved my sins. The coach was a gentle, unassuming man who was disarming. I instantly liked him and my decision to go to that school had more to do with what I saw in that man than anything else.

The school was about two hundred miles south of my hometown, so the next fall I moved away from home for the first time. When I got on campus, I suddenly realized that I didn't know how to act. I had never spent time exclusively with Christians my own age. Growing up I never went to youth group, and in my mind Christians weren't very cool (except me of course). When I arrived, I still chewed tobacco, slept with my girlfriend, was foul-mouthed, sharp-tongued, and incredibly selfish. I knew that some of these behaviors were forbidden at the school so I just kept them to myself.

We were expected to go to chapel during the week, which I thought was ridiculous, so I usually went back to my dorm room to sleep. One thing I couldn't avoid was my Bible survey classes and the associated homework. I had to read through the whole Bible. I also could not escape the mandatory Bible verse memory test my baseball coach required the team to pass before we could play. God's truth was reaching me and he powerfully used that faithful man in my life for two years. It did not take long for my sins to start eating at me.

It also did not take long for my depression to return. I remember the sinking feeling as my ability to complete schoolwork slowly dwindled. For some reason I had hoped I was done with all of that, like I had left it behind in my hometown. Completing daily tasks became overwhelming. I was barely getting by academically but God, in his goodness, brought another gentle, godly man into my life. My advisor and psychology professor had a gift for mentoring young men, and he quickly became a stabilizing influence in my life.

It was at this time that I first encountered Saint Augustine and his book *Confessions*. I was fascinated by his thorough examination of himself and his life. It had never occurred to me to examine my own life so closely. That book had a profound impact on me; after the Bible it has been the most influential book in my life by far.

As I began to develop self-awareness, I realized that I was extremely emotional and immature. I hated that about myself, but I had been that way as far back as I could remember. My peers didn't act the way I did, and I felt like I was on autopilot, stumbling through life without any understanding of why I was always so volatile. I had told off countless coaches and teachers. I was always embarrassed after these outbursts and would apologize, which I'm grateful to my parents for forcing me to do.

I was aggressive and competitive, but I also cried easily and often (still do). My whole life had been a constant search for consistency and stability. I badly needed people who provided clear expectations and structure. I decided that I wanted to become just like my baseball coach and psychology professor. These men were balanced, calm, gentle, and always under control. Through their actions and words, they testified that Jesus Christ was their Lord and King and they continually pointed me towards him. They followed Christ whereas I simply followed my own desires, a distinction I could not yet see.

As the semester went on, I kept getting exposed to the gospel. I could feel changes stirring within me. As my depression worsened, so did my growing guilt and shame over my continued sin. I knew that I needed to change, so I broke up with my girlfriend, removing that temptation. I felt a lot better about myself. In fact, I started thinking I was a pretty good person. I was oblivious to God's holiness and the depths of my sin. I had merely given up something that was making me feel guilty, but my heart had not changed.

The year was wrapping up and my roommate

asked if I would be a counselor at a local Christian summer camp. I agreed because I had nothing else to do and it sounded kind of fun and like something a Christian college student *should* do. When I set off for camp I realized that I could have my sin or follow Jesus but I couldn't have both." At that point it was clear to me that I had to truly repent, change, and leave my sins behind. With that knowledge, I chose Christ and decided that I would follow him wherever he led me. God had given me a new heart and I began a long, painful process of growth into a new man.

My first real growth as a believer, small as it was, happened over that summer. Early on at the camp all the staff gathered to pray for incoming campers and for all the general needs of the camp. It was scheduled for something like an hour and I was stunned by the sheer length. "Who prays for an hour? I will be bored after ten minutes at best." I had yet to encounter God's majesty in any meaningful way, but he was working in me. My mental health was pretty good that whole summer. I had to be in bed early and up early and I was busy all the time. I enjoyed the time with the campers and fellowship with the other counselors.

I returned to school with a new heart, but I was still incredibly immature. Consistent with my pattern, I started getting depressed early in the fall semester and remained pretty low until spring when baseball began. I struggled academically that entire year and felt so depressed and tired that the thought of being social overwhelmed me.

God, in his goodness, brought another stabilizing support into my life that year. A new student transferred to our small college. He was a few years older and as soon as we met, I could tell he was an interesting person with whom I would get along well. We quickly established a friendship that I credit with being one of the primary reasons I was able to finish college. My friend had come from very difficult circumstances, and God called him out of his situation and transformed him into a new man.

My remaining college years were more of the same. I was depressed each year generally from the end of September through late March. I had come to view depression as a part of my normal life. Something that would always be with me in some way. I struggled to get through my classes and my grades were never very good. Before I began my senior year I started thinking about life after college. I wanted to go to graduate school and I realized that I had to focus all my efforts on academics to try to improve my grades. I decided not to play baseball that year and spent the extra time studying. My grades improved, but it was also the first time, since I was 17, that the manic side of my mental illness returned. I had a hypomanic episode that lasted almost two months; I was less socially inhibited, drove recklessly, and stayed up all night reading novels. Hypomanic episodes are less severe and typically less impairing than full-blown manic episodes so sometimes they are difficult to recognize. In my case, I've always been odd so I think other people viewed my strange behavior during that time as a result of my quirky personality. No one, including me, recognized that I was having hypomanic episodes.

That spring, at the age of twenty-two, I graduated college with a degree in psychology. Without an advanced degree I couldn't do much in the field, but my grades were too poor for graduate school admission. It was at this point that I began to hunger for God's word and to understand it better. My father had attended seminary and I knew that his school had a master's degree program in counseling, it sounded like a good fit. I could get a better grounding in God's Word and get a graduate degree that I could use for a career in psychology. I contacted the seminary and told them that my grades didn't meet the entrance requirements but I asked if there was any way I could show them that I was capable of doing the work. The school graciously allowed me to begin taking classes with the incentive that if I got good grades they would consider letting me into the program. I will forever be grateful for that opportunity.

When I relocated for graduate school, I didn't know anyone in the city. I moved into a small apartment, where I lived a Spartan existence. I had a bed, a couch, and a small table in the kitchen, but my only place to sit was a plastic, folding lawn chair. A box of books provided a makeshift console for my small television. I typed my seminary papers while lying on the floor.

Because I was not yet in the counseling program, I started taking some of the requisite classes for the master's degree in divinity. For the first time, I was struck by God's majesty, holiness, and sovereignty. I constantly read about God's attributes and his great works throughout Scripture. I was coming to know him and recognizing how different I was from him. God showed me a glimpse of my sinfulness when I first became a Christian, but now I was forced to stare at myself in comparison to him—and it was ugly. I began praying in earnest that God would change me into a godly man and that he would show me more of himself.

I went to school during the day and worked part-time in the evenings. I tried a few different churches but never got connected. That fall I became severely depressed. I cried often, almost every time I was alone. I had been so mentally ill for so many years that I had chosen not to date. Frankly, I didn't have much to give another person.

I first met Bobbi Jo that September, when we were hired on the same day at the same company we continue to work for even today. I thought she was attractive and interesting and I could see by the thoughtful way she treated others that she was kind. After working together for nearly a year, I asked her a few times to go to coffee or lunch, but each time she declined. I assumed she had her reasons for refusing so I stopped asking. I still didn't know anyone in the city that I could hang out with but there was an attractive woman working on campus and one day I asked her if she would like to go out to dinner with me. We had a single date but didn't have much in common. A week later Bobbi Jo asked me if I had made any friends but before I could even answer, she said, "you know you should just go out on some dates." She then suggested I ask the woman I had gone out with the week prior. I told her that I recently had been out with her but I wasn't interested in going out with her again. Prior to that moment I really thought Bobbi Jo had no interest in me but her reaction was unmistakable. She was envious that I had been out with this other woman. I could tell that she was interested in me and I was very happy about it. A couple days later I asked Bobbi if she would go out to dinner with me and I was relieved when she finally agreed. We went out on a Friday night and I will never forget how I felt. It is still one of the happiest days of my entire life. During my years of depression, I struggled greatly engaging with people, so I had set myself to the careful study of others. Bobbi was everything I could have asked for: smart, funny, full of energy, devoted, loyal, gentle, and beautiful. I was captivated by this bold, strong woman. I wanted to learn everything there was to know about her. I had never met anyone like her before and I haven't since. After three months of dating, I asked her to marry me. I had no doubt that she was the right person for me. As the real severity of my mental health problems would reveal themselves over the first few years of our marriage, her unfailing commitment, strength, and devotion to me would prove that to be truer than I ever could have realized.

Brokenness

Before Micah and I married, I knew about his sister's sudden and tragic death when he was only 14, and I knew that exposure to trauma like that could have enduring consequences. I also knew a fair amount about the ensuing substance use issues he had struggled through during his adolescence. While no one yet understood that Micah had bipolar disorder, I knew he had a history of depression. He had been very honest and transparent with me and the red flags, so to speak, were all clearly visible. And even if they had not been, several people tried to warn me.

Each time I met one of Micah's former college

friends, they all had the same three-part reaction: First, they would look at Micah in disbelief that he was actually dating. Next, they would get excited and give both of us a big hug. Then later, privately, they would corner me with a serious look and say something along the lines of "Everyone loves Micah, really, he's a terrific guy, but are you sure you want to date him?" It was clear to me that his close friends loved him deeply and were very loyal to him; I wasn't sure which one of us they were trying to protect. When I met his family for the first time, I was shocked when even his mother pulled me aside and said, eyebrows raised, "I sure hope you know what you're getting into." At 24 years old, I surely did not.

I met Micah when we were both hired for similar research jobs. On the first day, our new supervisor told us to meet her at a restaurant for lunch. When Micah arrived, he caught my attention immediately. He was handsome, strong, and tanned, having spent the prior summer working on a roofing crew. I tried to get to know him over lunch, but he was quiet and revealed very little about himself. I knew only that he had recently moved to the area and had started a graduate program at a local seminary. I was also enrolled in graduate school, training to become a counselor. It was this mutual interest that had led us both to part-time work in mental health research.

We soon learned that we were going to be working on separate research projects but over the course of the next year we became close friends.

Part of our roles were to assess depressed adolescents to determine their risk of suicide. My desk was near Micah's and I learned so much from him and about him by listening as he spoke to teens and their parents on the phone. I was keenly impressed by his ability to build rapport quickly with very guarded, wounded young people. He used compassion and humor to coax them to open up about their private experiences. He listened thoughtfully and never judged them. He gently urged them to tell their story. Without ever disclosing his own experiences, just by the manner in which he asked them questions he was able to convey a sense of shared understanding. These youths trusted him, and so did their parents. In many cases the adolescents we interviewed had never been diagnosed with depression and we had to alert their parents not only that their child had a mood disorder but that they were also thinking about suicide. These were difficult conversations, but Micah handled them with grace. I was so impressed by his gentle nature.

Micah took his role seriously, but he didn't take himself too seriously. His playful and relaxed manner in the office was a huge encouragement to our co-workers during stressful times. For me, he was a gift I didn't know I needed. He was so different from me. He was calm and grounded, self-assured and secure with a quiet confidence that I longed for. I was ambitious and driven, but as a result over-involved in school and work, distracted, and moving in too many directions; so many that for several months I even failed to perceive that he was asking me out on dates. It took him asking someone else out on a date for me to come to my senses and realize that I was about to miss out on something. He loves to tell people how he recognized the jealousy in my face when he told me he had been out with someone else. I think we recognized it at the same moment, and I knew that he knew.

When we started dating, between school and work we were fairly busy during the week, so we made it a priority to go to church together and spent much of our weekends together. We had only dated for three months when Micah asked me to marry him. His proposal came earlier than I expected but I knew his heart, I could envision a future with him, and I had a strong sense that the Lord had led us to one another, and so in faith we began planning a wedding for the following summer. Our courtship was a time of relative health for Micah, but things began to change not long after we were married.

Our first year of marriage was exceptionally difficult for a number of reasons. We faced the typical adjustments newlyweds make as they learn to accommodate one another. Setting up house together that first summer we learned quickly that our organizational habits couldn't be more opposite. We also kept opposite schedules. Micah, having had years of difficulty sleeping, was in the habit of relaxing after work and then studying late into the night and sleeping late into the following morning. I, on the other hand, was early to bed and early to rise. This difference in routines caused a number of practical and romantic problems. I had to adjust to the idea of going to bed alone and had to give up my silly fantasy that we would be up at dawn for a sunrise run together before enjoying our morning coffee and newspaper. These expectations seem embarrassingly trivial as I write them now, but they demonstrate who I was at that time and what I thought our marriage would look like.

As summer turned to fall and the days grew darker, so did Micah's mood. At first I noticed that I was doing increasingly more than my share of house chores. Assuming that "the honeymoon was over," I regularly reminded him—he might say nagged—of our decision to divide housework evenly. These encouragements did little to motivate a change in his behavior, yet I persisted and as I did he withdrew. He began sleeping later and later into the day.

On weekends I would make plans for us to spend time together. When he would finally emerge from the bedroom, he would insist on working out for two hours at the gym. Again, I'm embarrassed to admit how much this annoyed me. I knew how important working out was to him, but I didn't yet understand how it provided so much mental health support to him. So I would wait, busying myself with other things until he returned—and then he often wouldn't be up for going out. It didn't take long before I began to resent him, concluding that he was lazy and selfish. I felt foolish for expecting him to be anything else and this led to a series of doubts about our compatibility and fears about how I could thrive in our marriage.

After we had been married almost two years I was in a car accident while waiting at a stop light just outside our offices. Someone took my driver's license to the building receptionist and returned with a very shaken-up Micah. I didn't realize at the time how much that accident frightened him. In retrospect, I can see it was a catalyst for our first experience of a hypomanic episode. We would come to discover later that serious life events would propel Micah toward mania.

A few weeks after the car accident, we got a phone call from our landlord announcing that she had decided to sell our rental house; we had 30 days to find a new place to live. We were both stunned. I had applied to and had been hearing back from doctoral programs but hadn't yet made a decision about where I wanted to attend school, which meant we could be moving and were in no position to consider purchasing a home. We needed to act quickly to find a new rental, so I told Micah we would discuss our options that evening. When I got home later, the dining room table was littered with house listings and realtor business cards. Before I could ask, Micah burst into the room talking rapidly on his cell phone. I listened to him confirm an appointment with a realtor to see a house. I couldn't believe what was happening. It had only been a couple of hours since we had gotten the news from the landlord. When he got off the phone Micah explained that he'd already lined up three showings for the next day. He wanted me to look at the fliers. I could see that some of the homes were well outside our means. I told him I thought he was jumping the gun. Insulted, he said that I didn't appreciate all the work he'd been through in the past few hours. He was outraged, a reaction I didn't expect.

This was the most energized I had ever seen him, and I didn't know what to make of it. It was a long night. He paced as I tried to calm him down and reassure him that we'd figure something out. I was reassuring myself just as much. It would be another year before we'd be in the midst of our first, full-blown manic episode, but this was a signal that something was very wrong. Though we didn't yet recognize it as hypomania, his behavior over the next few weeks was concerning enough that, after much grieving and prayer, I withdrew my applications and made the decision to attend a local graduate program so we could remain near our families in the event we needed their support to cope with whatever Micah was going through.

We bought a house. Almost a year later we had our first major home-repair experience. We had a beautiful, large Sitka spruce in our front yard that was more than one hundred years old. Its roots had penetrated our water main, causing a leak. I would have hired a contractor immediately, but Micah was convinced he could save us some money by digging the ditch himself and only bringing in someone to lay the new pipe and inspect it. I nervously watched him ramp up with that same determination and energy I'd seen the year before. He could not be dissuaded.

He borrowed my dad's truck and drove it recklessly all over town buying equipment we'd only use once and overbuying components for a sprinkler system he had spontaneously and unilaterally decided to install. "Well, we're halfway there with these ditches already dug," he explained when I saw him unloading enough PVC to outfit our entire neighborhood with underground watering systems. Just as with the real estate fliers the year before, he was annoyed that I didn't appreciate his great idea and the work he'd already put in, but he didn't let it deter him. One night, as the project was nearing completion, I collected broken sprinkler components that had been jettisoned randomly throughout the yard. I counted thirty-seven. I looked around. Our yard was completely trampled. I felt like it resembled my life.

That fall I started school. Micah's mood still hadn't righted itself. He avoided eye contact and was furtive. During that time, he would leave before dawn to go fishing; it became his obsession. After losing his wedding ring and the debacle that followed, I asked his parents to stay with us because I was worried about leaving him alone. One evening I had to leave for class and nobody had heard from Micah all day. He'd gone out before sunrise, and although we'd all tried calling him multiple times, he hadn't answered. His dad reassured me that Micah had probably lost his cell phone in the river and both his parents urged me to leave for school, promising to call as soon as he was home. I drove the forty-five minutes to campus, praying the entire way.

I might as well have stayed home because I certainly wasn't able to focus on the lecture that evening. I cannot describe the fear of wondering if your loved one is alive or dead. Another time, during a later episode, Micah again disappeared for an entire day. That time he came home with both wrists wrapped neatly in white gauze and surgical tape, I will never forget the terror that pulsed through my body when I saw those bandages. Fearing he had attempted suicide, you can imagine my relief when I learned that he had decided impulsively to have his wrists tattooed.

I mentioned earlier that I am a psychologist, so you might be wondering how I failed to recognize what was happening with my husband. It's a valid question, one I used to ask myself repeatedly in the aftermath of our first big manic episode. Here I was studying mental illness but

I couldn't see it right in front of me. I can only say that as a bystander or observer experiencing this illness for the first time, when mania arrived on the heels of depression, as it is often wont to do, I did not see it coming. Its onset and progression were rapid. I was so desperate for Micah's depression to be over that initially when he became more activated I was hopeful that his mood was finally lifting. At that time I didn't have any reason to suspect we would swing so far in the opposite direction. I had never been told about his manic episodes as an adolescent because up to that point nobody had recognized them as such. As a relatively new wife struggling in what felt like a horribly mismatched marriage, I had accommodated so many aspects of Micah's behavior in illness that I couldn't see things for what they were. When Micah became angry and selfish I recalled how he had shared with me the person he had been before we met and I came to think that I was immature and was to blame for expecting him to be any different. The truth is, when you are in the midst of these kinds of experiences, for the first time, it can be hard to see things clearly, even when you know something is terribly wrong.

When he finally agreed to see a psychiatrist, Micah was diagnosed with bipolar disorder, which was as hard to accept as it was to deny. He was immediately prescribed medication to arrest the manic episode we were enduring. His psychiatrist asked us if we wanted her to recommend hospitalization. Micah was strongly motivated to avoid inpatient treatment, so I agreed to administer his medications at home even though I wasn't sure going home a good idea.

Before we left her office, the doctor asked me if I had any additional concerns. Because she wanted to respect Micah above all, she left me only a few minutes to talk at the end of the appointment. Her matter-of-fact manner left me feeling like she didn't fully comprehend what we had been going through. I tried to describe for her the events that led us there. I told her about the reckless driving and spending, the relentless fishing and lack of sleep, Micah's complete disregard for anyone else's feelings or safety. I'm not sure what my goal was, but I felt she needed to know everything so that she could properly treat Micah.

I wanted her to be as alarmed as I was. I wanted her to validate my feelings. I was desperate for the madness to end and I was exhausted. She asked Micah if he would consider surrendering his credit cards and keys to me until he was in better shape. Both of us felt uncomfortable with this idea. It is a very awkward situation to parent your adult partner and try to respect him at the same time. He grudgingly handed them over and I reluctantly accepted them. "Anything else?" she asked me. I told her that he wanted to paint the interior of our living room and she said "Great! Let him! That sounds like a great way to burn out some of that excessive energy." I stared back at her in disbelief. Clearly, my account of our harrowing experiences had not been compelling or vivid enough. She had no idea what a disaster it would be to give Micah a can of paint in his state. The ceilings, electric sockets, fireplace, rugs, wall sconces, wood floors, they would all end up lacquered. I wanted to be taken seriously. I wanted a new doctor. But Micah liked her and because he liked her, he filled the prescription she had written and I decided that would have to be victory enough.

We returned home not sure what to expect next. I felt the tremendous burden of being his care provider when I knew he belonged at the hospital. When someone is acutely manic, the medication protocol to disrupt the mania is different than the one to maintain a stable mood. Sometimes the medications are actually different; other times the doses are just more powerful. These medications are intended to halt the body so the mind can rest and restore. The longer mania progresses the harder it can be to bring it to an end. This particular episode had persisted for some time, so the initial doses were ineffective. We had to greatly increase both his antipsychotic medication and his mood stabilizer, which left him so heavily sedated that I felt that I needed to stay constantly by his side; I was literally afraid he would stop breathing and so even when he was resting I felt I needed to stay awake. It's difficult to write this now as I think about the shell of the woman who sat at his bedside, so depleted and frightened and trying to handle so much on her own. Of course if the medications had put him at risk for respiratory depression his doctor would have insisted he be in the hospital for monitoring but I share this story to demonstrate how little I knew about the treatments and their effects. I was a 26-year-old, first-year doctoral student with hardly any training about psychotropic medications. I felt alone and terrified at how out of control our situation had become. I was so sleep deprived I was no longer thinking clearly, I wasn't able to care for myself, and our lives were completely upside down.

Micah shuffled around in a stupor for weeks. In total it would take six full months for him to recover. It was so hard to see my formerly handsome, strong husband transform. He fell asleep at the table with food falling out of his mouth. He drooled. He grew puffy in the face and gained thirty-five pounds in a few months (weight gain is a common side effect of antipsychotic medications). His eyes were distant and glazed. He couldn't carry on a conversation and muttered unintelligibly to himself. I wondered if this was the way our life was to be.

I felt I had traded one nightmare for another. No one told me that once the mania was fully over, his medications would be adjusted again, nor did I realize that adjusting medications would become a part of our lives from that time forward, or that we might find a set of medications and doses that worked for a while only to suddenly stop working or become less effective for no apparent reason. Many of the medications that are used in psychiatry aren't precise tools. These aren't drugs that were developed based on an understanding of the brain mechanisms that underlie mood disorders or psychosis; rather, these are medications that, in many cases, were accidentally discovered to treat these conditions.

We would be back in the psychiatrist's office several times over the following weeks and months, adjusting medications and doses until Micah was eventually able to establish a reasonably stable mood. Finding the right treatment takes time; people react differently to medications, they metabolize them differently, and side effects that are unbearable for one person may not affect the next person. Benefits of the medications used to treat serious mental illnesses come at a tremendous cost to the person taking them, and it can take time for a person to decide if they are willing to tolerate the side effects or if they need to try another medication or dose. Many people discontinue medications because of intolerable side effects.

Micah's psychiatrist advised and worked patiently with us, and over time I came to appreciate her. I learned so much by watching her interact with my husband. She was never alarmed, I assume because in her many years of practice, she'd seen it all. She was always steady. She always spoke directly to Micah. She took time to educate him about his choices. She always asked him how he felt about the decisions they were making, and he always had a say. She would ask me as well. We grew to trust her immensely; she helped us put our life back together. We were devastated when she retired and felt so fortunate when his next psychiatrist was equally compassionate and competent.

Micah and I remember very little of the next few years. I think we were barely surviving. I was going to graduate school and working full time; he was working full time when he could. He had several more episodes, alternating between mania and depression, sometimes cycling quickly between the two, sometimes experiencing episodes that were a mix of both. He wrestled with substance use problems that came with manic episodes. He wrestled through a difficult work situation with a supervisor who was unaccommodating and unsympathetic to his mental health needs. During that time he received corrective action and feared he would lose his job, adding more strain to an already very stressful situation.

Micah very likely would have been fired if it had not been for one person. Coincidentally, at the time of his first adult episode of mania, Micah was working on a research project interviewing people about their experiences living with illnesses like bipolar disorder and schizophrenia. The researcher who led this work had spent years developing a model of recovery from serious mental illnesses, and through this work, she became sensitive to the ways that mental health problems can disrupt life goals, including the pursuit of meaningful work. After his diagnosis, as Micah continued to have trouble meeting his work obligations, instead of documenting evidence of his poor performance as grounds for termination, as his supervisor was doing, this mentor took time to talk with him about the problems he was having and how they were affecting the work of the research team. This wasn't meant to burden Micah or make him feel guilty; instead it was meant to help him remember that he was an integral part of the team and that the team needed and wanted to support him so they could resume their important work together.

She and Micah had many difficult conversations—she would hold Micah accountable for problems that resulted from his lack of concentration or disorganized thinking. He respected her and he would accept responsibility without blaming his illness (even when it was largely to blame), which she respected. The two worked together to come up with reasonable accommodations so Micah could continue to do his work. Not only did he maintain his job, but eventually, as he gradually resumed his mental health, because of the support of this person he was able to be promoted to a position where he could better use his skills. He is now a significant contributor to our research portfolio and his personal experiences living with a mental illness make him an invaluable asset to our work.

Illness
Defined

I don't recall much about my life between the ages of twenty-five and thirty-two. Rather than linear memories, I have disjointed "flashbulb" recollections from those years. I was constantly sick throughout that time, either depressed, hypomanic, manic, or attempting to recover from any of these. Over that seven-year period I had seven severe episodes of depression, four manic episodes, and two mixed episodes (when I was simultaneously depressed *and* hyperactive, needing much less sleep). I never went to the hospital, but I should have on at least a few occasions. I was a near constant danger to myself and at times to others.

With each passing year I became less functional and noticed increasingly more cognitive impairment as constant illness tore my mind apart. I couldn't think as well as I had before. I was easily confused and forgetful. Simple tasks became difficult. At a couple of points, I thought I would no longer be able to work because I could not stay well. Because I feared losing my job, I focused all my energy on my performance at work, but outside of the job I had become almost incapable of social interaction. I know it was often embarrassing for Bobbi when we went to social gatherings because I was awkward, cold, and unfriendly. I am sure we appeared to be one of those terribly mismatched couples.

I felt like I was always behind and either depression or mania was always ahead. I couldn't seem to land between the two. I would be so impaired from one episode that the next easily overwhelmed me when it came. And that's how I lived, back and forth, up and down. People who have never experienced or cared for someone with bipolar disorder have a hard time understanding what this illness is like. There are a lot of misconceptions and, frankly, not everyone experiences bipolar disorder in the same way. In the following section, I describe my experiences using symptoms and terms described in the *Diagnostic and Statistical Manual of Mental Disorders,* 5th edition *(American Psychiatric Association, 2013),* or DSM-5. This is a manual that provides guidelines for diagnosing mental illnesses. According to this manual, my experiences meet the criteria for what is described as bipolar I disorder, which means that I have full manic episodes and full major depressive episodes.

MANIA

Elevated, expansive, or irritable mood. The term bipolar leads people to assume that mania must be the opposite of depression – so it must mean being really happy or hyper. But just like depression is not only experienced as sadness (for example, I often experience a lack of sadness or any emotion), mania is not only experienced as euphoria and elevated mood. I have felt euphoric when I've been manic, but irritability stands out more because it is so miserable. Euphoria feels really good. Everything around me seems more intense. The world around me looks more vivid, lights seem brighter than normal, and sounds seem crisper and louder. At times it feels like the world around me is a fantastic dream; I feel almost intoxicated by the feelings, sights and sounds.

When I encounter barriers to accomplishments I feel driven to attain during this period, I get extremely irritable, such as when I have to stay home with no access to money and no transportation. I have all this energy and internal drive, but I'm stuck in the house so instead I pace restlessly for hours.

While I am either euphoric or irritable during my manic episodes I also have one- to two-day periods where I am almost catatonic (although I still don't need much sleep). I will have been going one hundred miles an hour for a week or more with very little sleep and constant racing thoughts when my mind "crashes" and I can't think at all. I become lost in an internal world and I am confused and delusional. I have trouble processing what people say. Then I bounce right back to euphoria or irritability, my mind is racing, and I feel driven to do things once again.

When I get irritable during mania, I become aggressive, demanding, hostile, impatient, and inconsiderate, nothing like my usual laid-back demeanor. This irritability typically lasts for a couple of days before swinging back toward euphoria and, if not arrested by medication, this pendulum swing continues for months. It feels like a relentless force within me, thrusting my mood upward until my mind is burned up and can't process anymore. Unmedicated, I can go through this process for two to three months. When it is finally over it feels as if I've lived an entire year in that time and can take more than six months for me to recover. I never feel depressed when I'm in a manic episode (this is different from a mixed episode in which I experience mania and depression simultaneously).

Decreased need for sleep. Unlike when I'm healthy, during episodes of mania I need very little sleep while still having unlimited energy during the day. Even fully medicated at acute treatment levels (which involve higher doses of medication intended to stop the mania) I never sleep more than two hours, usually from two o'clock to four o'clock a.m., and I awake full of energy. During one episode I thought I should probably try to get a little sleep. I fell asleep pretty quickly, but about a half an hour later, I shot out of bed with a sensation of electricity coursing through my body.

The human body can't endure with so little sleep for long, so eventually I fall asleep from exhaustion in the middle of the day, seemingly without warning. Once, while I was experiencing a manic episode, I was waiting in the pharmacy to pick up a new medicine. I had not slept for two days and I was very irritable because the pharmacy was extremely busy and I was going to have to wait. I sat down and the next thing I knew, the pharmacy was almost completely empty. I looked at my phone and I realized that I had been asleep for almost two-and-a-half hours.

More talkative than usual or pressure to keep talking. During my first adult manic episode, I essentially took over a meeting at work. I talked over anyone who tried to participate in the conversation. I had ideas about how our department should be reorganized and how we might more efficiently do our work, and I laid out my grand plans. When a co-worker spoke up to disagree, I jumped down her throat. The room fell silent. Another co-worker who was also a friend tried to intervene, but I was oblivious to my disrespectful and disruptive behavior.

These experiences are some of the most difficult to recover from because when you later realize how you have behaved in front of others you feel humiliated. It's important to me that I assume responsibility for my behavior, even when it is a result of being sick, so I always try to make amends later, and sometimes people are forgiving and gracious.

During another episode years later, that same friend, who was by this time aware of my illness, alerted Bobbi Jo that he thought I should probably leave work before I was asked to leave. I had been pacing around the office all morning, talking a mile a minute about various things, barely letting anyone get a word in edgewise and not letting anyone get any work done. Bobbi found me in a hallway where I had cornered a small group of people, telling them an unending story. I couldn't be torn away. I was reciting movie lines, telling bad jokes, jumping from one topic to the next and laughing hysterically at myself, oblivious to the nervous laughter of my audience. It took Bobbi two hours to get me out of that hallway.

Racing thoughts and distractibility. When I'm manic, my mind jumps from one big idea to the next and I am rarely able to focus on one thing for long. I concoct grand ideas for projects but rarely get past the starting phase before I lose interest and move on, with intensely driven energy, to something new. During one manic episode, for example, I got it in my head that I would make a short stop-action film using my children's action figures and toys. I got a bunch of them set up and then meticulously took pictures, adjusting and repositioning the characters before each frame. The next day I forgot all about it, having moved on to the next big project. Some of those pictures still exist, and Bobbi and I have to laugh when we come across them because it looks like the work of small children.

Another time I had a brilliant idea to create a timeline of church history on giant pieces of paper. It was going to be amazing and so detailed that seminaries would want to use it for training students. I passionately sold the idea to Bobbi Jo and became upset when she failed to show the enthusiasm I expected. I never actually started making the timeline and soon forgot about it.

Because I'm easily distracted, I have difficulty blocking out competing stimuli. It can be overwhelming to be somewhere with lots of people talking, particularly because I have a hard time ignoring their conversations. It's as though my mind attempts to simultaneously hear and process all of the discussions at once. When it's happening, I feel as if it is tearing my mind apart, but I can't keep from doing it.

Increase in goal-directed behavior. There are a few things I have been consistently driven to do during manic episodes. One of these is lifting weights. I enjoy working out when I'm well and weightlifting has always been part of managing my mental health. However, when I'm manic, I become obsessed with it. I work out for hours every day, and because I get very little sleep, my body can't adequately heal. As a result, I usually feel physically broken down when the manic episodes ends. Bobbi's best friend has a favorite memory of going to the gym with us while I was manic; apparently I took it upon myself to be Bobbi's trainer that day and my expectations for her workout were ridiculously unrealistic. I'm glad the memory brings her friend joy and we can all laugh about it now.

Another thing I've been obsessed with during manic episodes has been tattoos. I have five of them on my arms, all of which I've gotten while manic. If Bobbi Jo had not intervened in most of my plans for tattoos, I'm pretty confident much of my body would be covered in ink. For some reason I fixate on the idea of having a new tattoo and when I'm sick I enjoy the physical pain involved.

Excessive involvement in potentially dangerous activities. I have also wanted to drive fast and to fish during my manic episodes, which has led to instances where I could have easily been killed or harmed someone else. Unfortunately, my judgment becomes so severely impaired that I fail to appreciate consequences or the dangerousness of my behavior.

One of my clearest memories of God's providential care for me occurred while I was out fishing. I had been going to a place where the river split and I could wade across to the middle section, where the fishing was better. It had always been difficult to get across safely, but the night before had seen heavy rains and the water level had risen significantly. I definitely underestimated the risk. I had my boots and hip waders on so I confidently went into the current, but before I even got to the middle, I was lifted off my feet and pulled downriver. Just a short way ahead the river narrowed, got deeper, and sped up considerably. With my boots and waders on, I had very little chance of surviving the rapids. Luckily another fisherman saw me, waded out as far as he safely could, and caught my arm as I rushed by. It nearly pulled him in, too, but with his help I was able to get my feet underneath me and steady us both. That man saved my life.

After my sanity returned, I came across the waders I had been wearing that day. They clearly looked too small, so I put them on to see. Skintight, they had to stretch considerably at the crotch since I was much too tall for them. I realized that I had owned them since I was a young teenager. I must have looked ridiculous out on the river. I wonder what other fishermen thought when they saw me strutting about confidently in my boots, fishing vest, and tiny waders. I have to find humor in some of these situations. During another manic episode I lost my driver's license (actually, that's happened more than once). It was the middle of winter and I didn't want to look pale in my replacement photo, so I borrowed some of Bobbi's self-tanning lotion. I didn't have any prior experience with tanning lotions and didn't realize that there are different tanners for face and body, that some are darker shades meant for later summer use, or that they continue to darken over time. I may have overdone it on the application, but I thought I looked pretty good, so I went to the DMV and got a new license. Later, once I had recovered from that episode, I laughed at the unnaturally orange face with a goofy smile printed on my license. I lost that license during a later episode.

Psychotic thinking. It is not unusual for me to have delusional thoughts or to become paranoid when I am manic. Frequently, I have been convinced that people could see me through my computer or television screens. I would watch TV far off to one side of the room so I was never right in front of the screen. In most, if not all, of my manic episodes, I have struggled with the belief that Bobbi was having an affair and because I was so out of my mind I had missed warning signs of her infidelity. I can usually find the seeds of my delusions in my healthy mind. My wrong belief about Bobbi's unfaithfulness obviously had seeds in a fear of abandonment and the loss of the person who is most important to me.

One recurring delusion I have had is the belief that I don't actually exist. It is hard to explain, but when I get really sick, my memories are distorted, my mind is racing, things around me seem surreal, and I get this idea that I am not actually here. From that point all kinds of strange and troubling ideas pour into my mind, greatly exacerbating my mental health problems. It's terrifying to be in a state where you truly believe you don't exist and the world around you isn't real. It's so distressing that I avoid everyone and everything in a frantic effort to hide away from it. There is often this not fully formed idea that if certain unidentified people learned I've become aware that I'm not real there could be some danger. My mind is malfunctioning so badly when I'm manic that even my delusions are incomplete ideas and the content is often inconsistent. During one of my manic episodes, I decided to write down the content of these delusions. When my sanity was slowly returning, I looked at the things I had written and none of it made any sense. The writing was almost incomprehensible, and the content was really weird. I thought about keeping it as a window into my state of mind when I'm manic but I'm thankful that I wisely deleted it from my computer. Seeing concrete evidence of my mental state when I'm manic, once I'm fully sane again, is very painful.

In the past it was hard to admit to myself how sick I was, so I ignored or minimized troubling experiences. I couldn't bear the thought of those things being true of me. I was always determined to fight my way out these episodes and press on. Admitting the truth made it hard to hold on to my hope of getting better. Now that I am healthier, it is much easier to see some these impairments more clearly.

The worst symptom—the signal of a mood transition. I experience a miserable sensation during transitions from depression to mania or vice versa. It is an internal disquiet, a terrible restlessness. It is not agitation, akathisia (a similar kind of internal restlessness, often induced my antipsychotic medications), anxiety, or irritability. I know what each of those things are and what they feel like. This is different, it's a gnawing internal state that feels awful. When it becomes constant and exceedingly intense, it is always a signal to me that something is starting to go awry; it is a warning to pay close attention to my mood and my thoughts. I know that I have to endure the feeling; I've found no way to relieve it. It feels inescapable and unbearable until I transition to either depression or mania when the sensation finally abates.

MAJOR DEPRESSIVE EPISODE

Depression

As with mania, clinical descriptions of depression with checklists of symptoms don't capture my experience. The best way I can describe the impending dread of depression and its lonely misery is through metaphor.

Imagine you are on a large ship at sea. You are sailing along in life but at some point you notice something is not quite right. Your ship has slowed considerably. You go below deck and find that the ship is taking on water, but you can't tell exactly how it is getting in. You check the normal trouble spots and find that water is coming through in a couple of places. You desperately work to plug the leaks, but just as quickly as you can make repairs, new leaks appear.

You've had a lot of practice stopping these leaks in the past and know that sometimes, if you work hard enough, you can keep the ship afloat. But the water is coming in fast and a feeling of dread washes over you as the situation gets out of control. You go up on deck to see that your ship is listing to one side and has completely stopped. You say, "Not again. Please not again, don't let this be happening again." But you know it is too late and you know what is coming next. Your ship is sinking and it is a long, long way to the bottom.

The water gets colder and darker as you descend. At the bottom you feel as if it will be impossible to ever raise your ship again. Then you remember that, with help, you have made it up from the bottom before. You know this is how life goes—you have to be strong enough to weather the hazards and inevitable storms. But you feel like you just got back from here. Then you remember how many times you have sunk. You know that your life will begin to pass you by and things will be left undone, words unsaid. You know that some people will think you are lazy or not trying hard enough to lift yourself and some will even think your sin in some way brought you down and keeps you here. You begin to think that this is actually where you belong, like something is inherently wrong with your ship and that it will never properly float again.

Depressed mood and lack of pleasure. I have cumulatively spent more than a third of my life depressed. The most distinct symptoms of my depression are down mood and the complete loss of the ability to enjoy anything (technically called anhedonia). Many people equate depression with sadness, and while I sometimes feel sad, most of the time I don't experience any emotions at all when I'm depressed. I feel cold, distant from everything around me, emotionally dead inside. This melancholy is actually physically painful at times.

When I am depressed, I am unable to find pleasure in any activities. It's not that I have a bad attitude or am being negative—I simply can't physically derive pleasure from anything. Hobbies I typically enjoy— fishing, lifting weights, bird watching, reading, talking with my wife, playing with my kids, woodworking, playing golf—are neither enjoyable nor fun when I'm depressed.

Appetite and weight change. I always lose my appetite when I get really depressed and I generally lose weight. In addition to feeling little desire for food, I also don't enjoy eating and food seems tasteless, which leads to weight loss. Other people experience increased appetite and weight gain when depressed.

Insomnia and fatigue. Because significant sleep problems are a constant in my life, not much changes when I get depressed. The only thing that allows me to sleep is medication that completely sedates me. When I'm depressed, I feel physically exhausted all of the time, no matter how much rest or sleep I get.

Persistent pessimism and feelings of worthlessness. When I'm depressed, I feel a strong almost irresistible pull to think negatively about nearly everything. I have sudden automatic thoughts about myself like "I am failure as father and husband." These are called cognitive distortions. I have learned to manage and refute these thoughts, but they still come to mind and I have to be vigilant to push them out or to reframe them to be more accurate and realistic. The combination of depressed mood, fatigue, and slow thinking often leave me feeling as if I am unable to love my wife adequately, show my children the attention and love they need, or do my job well. These feelings of worthlessness increase the temptation to despair, remind me of all my past failures, and begin to generate an intense feeling of guilt within me. I have to fight hard against all of this.

Concentration impairment. As when I am manic, I have difficulty concentrating when I am depressed, but instead of struggling to limit interference of irrelevant stimuli, I struggle to think clearly. My thinking becomes muddled and slow and I have trouble persisting in thought. I am also far more forgetful than normal when I am depressed.

Suicidal thoughts. I used to think about ending my life. While I still have disturbing intrusive thoughts of suicide, particularly when I am depressed and getting a little delusional and paranoid, I do not want to harm myself, and therefore I don't entertain these thoughts. I try to push them aside as quickly as they arise. For more about how I manage suicidal thoughts, see "Addressing Suicide" at the end of this book.

Returning to the metaphor, my thoughts are bleak, confused, and distorted when I'm at the bottom. But something surprising can happen down there. When everyone feels impossibly far away and the blessings of this world are muted, God, speaking through his Word, is crystal clear. When it seems that nothing can reach me, God can because his word "is living and effective and sharper than any double-edged sword, penetrating as far as the separation of soul and spirit, joints and marrow" (Heb 4:12). His Word cuts through the depths and the darkness directly to my heart. God's Word becomes this bright light within the darkness that shines the light of life in my life and exposes the distorted thoughts and lies that fill my mind in that lonely empty place.

It is miserable at the bottom, but in all the time I have spent there God has always been with me, and his merciful presence has forced me to depend on him alone. Each time I've sunk to the depths my love for him has deepened out of my great thankfulness for his kindness. This process doesn't happen automatically. I have to tell myself that God's Spirit actually dwells within me (2 Cor. 1:21; Rom. 8:9; Eph. 1:13). I have to tell myself to trust him and wait for him, down there seemingly all alone. I have to tell myself to listen hard to the muffled voices of his servants who are in my life. I tell myself to accept their help and utilize the tools of modern medicine while I wait. I have to force myself to attend church and listen to his word preached each week. I have to continue to read his word each day. I have to call out to him regularly in prayer. It's almost impossible to enjoy anything at the bottom; the smallest burdens feel insurmountable but amazingly I am able to read God's word and praying brings contentment and peace. I can actually experience joy in that cold dark place but it is the joy that can only come through Christ, the wellspring of life (John 4:14).

A Decision to Change

The cycle of massive swings from depression to mania and back again that had been going on for seven years changed as a result of a manic episode that caught me completely off guard at age thirty-two. In the months leading up to that episode, I thought I was getting a handle on managing my illness, but I got complacent and stopped paying close attention to warning signs. That episode was devastating in a number of ways that forced me to take a hard look at my illness, my faith, my marriage, and myself. There were two specific incidents that deeply affected me and I mulled them over repeatedly in the months following the episode, while I was recovering. In many ways these experiences became the catalyst that fueled a desperate internal drive to get well and stay well, no matter what.

The first experience was my son's second birthday party. Like many two-year-old boys, he loved fire trucks. Bobbi and her mother had coordinated with the local fire department to have his birthday party at the firehouse. I was near the middle of what would turn out to be my last manic episode, and I hadn't been going out into public except to the gym, but I knew I could not miss this event. I felt like an absent father showing up to his son's birthday party, a stranger. For obvious reasons our two children were never left alone in my care and someone was always around when I spent time with them. The only exception was when I was able to swaddle our younger infant daughter at night, feed her a bottle, and rock her back to sleep while my wife slept. I had never done this with our son because I had been so sick so consequently he was not very attached to me. He was now two and this birthday was a stark reminder of my failures. I felt so much sadness over being so sick when my kids needed me so badly.

All the way to the fire station, I kept telling myself to stay calm and in control. I felt terribly afraid of how I would act and what others would think. The families coming, some of our closest friends, knew I was sick, but most had probably never seen me while I was manic. My son was delighted by all the fire trucks, the firemen, and their equipment. For me, the whole experience was intensely painful and one of those brief moments in mania when my mind cleared enough for me to see, at least to some degree, what a wreck I was. I tried so hard to be present during the party, but I felt like crying the entire time. I felt as if everyone were staring at me, like they knew how crazy I was. I knew they must have felt so sorry for Bobbi and our children. I worked hard at holding all of this inside my head and tried to act normal.

For the rest of that episode I spent a lot of time with our children while they slept. I didn't need much sleep, so I would lie beside his bed or her crib. I would pray for them and ask God to enable me to be a good father. I would also sing softly to them since it was hard to keep myself from talking in some way. Because I could never sit still for long, I would pace around the house, then come back to their rooms and listen to them sleep some more. I treasured those moments because I knew I couldn't disappoint or harm them.

As that last full manic episode was slowly ending, I had a second experience that, in retrospect, appears small but felt profound. Our daughter was four months old and on this particular day we were out of diapers. Because Bobbi was completing her predoctoral internship that year, she was making very little money. I had been on temporary disability and earned a fraction of my normal income. Bobbi had asked me to adjust my spending and eventually had to ask me to give up access to our accounts. I had been so self-absorbed during the episode that I was unaware of our financial state.

Because Bobbi was literally sick with exhaustion and because I was getting better, she asked me to go to the store to pick up diapers. She gave me my debit card and car keys for this shopping trip. When I tried to pay for the diapers my card was declined. I took it to the nearby ATM to get cash but was declined again. I called Bobbi and she immediately called the bank to learn that our account was overdrawn. Bobbi called ahead to our credit union and had a check drawn from our savings for me to pick up. I took it to our bank for deposit, thinking I could get some cash back to buy the diapers, but the hold on our account would remain for a couple more days and the bank teller refused to give me any cash.

Nothing like this had ever happened to me before. I felt mortified. I called Bobbi from the car to tell her what had happened. True to form, she told me to wait in the car while she took care of things. In almost no time, she called to ask me to return to the bank and talk to the same teller who denied my request for cash. When I did, the woman was apologetic and gave me the cash that I needed. Even after all I had put Bobbi through over the prior months she called me back to apologize for not realizing that our account was overdrawn. She knew I was discouraged and embarrassed and she tried to encourage me.

As I thought about this experience and Bobbi's gracious attitude, I saw that she had been working full time, finishing her dissertation in her "free" time, nursing an infant every two hours, raising an active two-year-old, and caring for a very sick husband. I should have been in the hospital and Bobbi knew it, but she also knew I was terrified of being admitted to inpatient treatment so she was enduring much suffering for my sake. As my mind began to clear I could see that she was exhausted, broken, and alone because I left her that way. I could never admit it before, but at some point that summer, I confessed to God that I had completely failed as a husband.

I had not loved my wife well enough, nor sacrificed for her, nor encouraged her in the Word. I knew that I had to confess this to Bobbi Jo as well and ask for her forgiveness. I also knew that these words would be empty and meaningless unless I showed my contrition and faithfulness to her through serving her in love as I should have from the day we got married.

I was failing at the primary roles God had given me in this life. He broke me in that episode of madness. My mind had been more broken before but not my heart, spirit, pride, rebelliousness, and selfishness. He crushed those things in me and I felt exposed and helpless. I had nothing to lean on but him. I was like a stranger to my children, my marriage was a mess, I did not know if I would be able to keep my job, my mind was severely impaired by years of constant illness, and I knew there was no guarantee that I would not lose my sanity again in the future. I was forced to look at myself and I could plainly see how helpless I was.

Inside all I saw was ruin, but outside I saw blessing and opportunity. I had a beautiful, gifted, kind, and patient wife; two joyous blessings in my children; a home; and, for the moment, a job. God broke me of just about everything except the tenacity he gifted in me. I had not given up yet, and I knew I would keep fighting, but I knew I had to trust his ways. I had to acknowledge that he would be the one to do this work inside of me.

I was failing, but he is a loving father who delights in reconciling and restoring relationships and making things new. He could make me a gentle, loving father who was intimately involved in the physical and spiritual lives of his children. He could make me a husband who served and sacrificially loved his wife. I knew this is what he had called me to, so I earnestly sought and depended on him to make those things happen. In this way he would show me that it was his good work—and not mine—and I would give him glory and praise him for his goodness.

This started a slow process of realizing that I had to take drastic steps to safeguard my health. I didn't want to be a father who was constantly sick.

I didn't want my children to see me change to a different person then disappear for a while so I could recover in the hospital. I didn't want to leave them confused by my sudden lifelessness and withdrawal in depression. I knew that I had to do whatever it took to get well and stay well.

Over the next year, I established a number of boundaries and rules for myself to monitor and take care of my health. For example, I set a rule that I would never get out of bed later than 7:00 a.m. no matter what. I knew fighting the sedation of my medications would be difficult, but I was determined. Every day, as soon as my alarm went off, I forced myself out of bed. I could hardly open my eyes or stand up very well; sometimes I would stumble out of my room, but nevertheless I did it every day. I knew I needed to do this for my health and for the kids, but primarily I did this out of love for Bobbi Jo. I wanted her to see this action, among other things, as a sign of how much I loved her. It probably sounds terribly unromantic to say I started getting up early every day out of love for my wife, but it was a sacrifice.

I gave up everything unnecessary that could in any possible way contribute to mania or distract me from noticing its warning signs. I decided that I had to be okay with giving up all my comforts, hobbies, and interests if that's what it would take to get well, stay well, and love my family well. I am not advising that anyone else with bipolar disorder should imitate me; I'm just reporting what I felt I needed to do.

I had always loved to escape into a good book, but I stopped reading novels since they were by definition fiction. I had to keep my mind in here-and-now reality. I also stopped watching movies almost entirely, especially ones that were overly stimulating or mind-bending in any way. I stopped watching sports because of the stress inherent in following my favorite teams. I also stopped paying close attention to politics.

I liked to daydream, but I set to work cutting off all unreal thoughts, thinking too far into the future, or allowing myself to think about regrets. I had to examine my mental, emotional, and spiritual state every single day in the light of reality. I also knew that I had to start telling Bobbi Jo about my internal struggles and any strange thoughts, even though they embarrassed me. I was so used to keeping my delusions to myself that I had to learn how to communicate things I had never verbalized before. I didn't want to acknowledge how weak and impaired I was, and I didn't want Bobbi to know how often I struggled. But the more I did, the easier it became, and my health slowly improved. Getting on an effective combination of medications was essential.

Getting Well and Staying Well

While I have found medication to be a necessary component of treatment, psychiatric drugs alone are not sufficient. Over time I have learned strategies that work for me to manage mania and depression when I am sick and prevent recurrence of them once I am well.

STRATEGIES FOR MANAGING ACUTE MANIA

Once a manic episode is in full swing, it is difficult to arrest, so my main goals are to adjust my medications and stay out of trouble.

I give up my car keys and agree not to drive. Because I am a near constant danger to myself and others and I don't properly evaluate risk or think ahead as I normally would, I just surrender my driving privileges. I once totaled a car, and thankfully no one was hurt. Instead if I need to go somewhere, someone has to drive me.

I avoid social commitments. When I'm manic I don't pick up on social cues well. For example, when people are alarmed or annoyed at my behavior, it is hard to filter my thoughts, so I say inappropriate or rude things that I would never speak aloud if I were well. This leads to embarrassment and can be hurtful to others.

I give up all access to money—cash, credit cards, debit cards. I agree not to purchase anything because my judgment is impaired. In the past I have made unwise decisions that had lasting financial consequences.

I meditate on Scripture and try to focus my attention on the Lord. I have difficulty reading and taking in new information when I am sick, so spending time in the Word is difficult, but I can reflect on passages of Scripture I have memorized.

After suffering several terrible episodes, I eventually learned that meditating on the Lord is my greatest refuge when I am sick. He is the only sure thing to hold on to.

I try to think about God and direct every stream of thought to him in some way—who he is, his attributes, what he has done, and the promises of what he will do. I know there is safety and reality in him and in meditating on who he says he is in the Word. He remains the same, even in my storms of madness. Everything else seems different and confusing, but he is not. He is good when I am sick, and he is good when I am well.

I now agree hospitalization, if necessary. In order to protect myself and my family—and to avoid my children witnessing my erratic and unusual behavior—I have agreed that I will go to the hospital if Bobbi tells me that's what we should do. I trust Bobbi Jo and my psychiatrist and have given advance directives to invoke hospitalization when necessary.

STRATEGIES FOR PREVENTING MANIA

I pay very close attention to six vital indicators that can signal whether mania or a mixed episode is approaching.

How well am I sleeping? A decreased need for sleep is one of the biggest signs that I am beginning to move toward mania, so I try to go to bed within the same two-hour window each night and wake up the same time each day. If I notice changes in how long it takes me to fall asleep or if I am waking more than once at night or if I am waking up an hour or more before my alarm, I pay closer attention to other parts of my life. If I experience a change in my sleeping pattern for a couple of nights, I don't worry too much about it. But if a change occurs on more than three consecutive nights, I start looking at steps I might need to take to get my sleep routine under control.

How well are my medications working? I always feel some level of sedation from my medications during the day, so I assess how sedated I feel when I wake up, during the afternoon, and at night. If, when I check in with myself, my level of sedation seems pretty normal or slightly worse than normal, I don't worry, but if I notice that I feel *less* sedated than normal at those three points in the day, then I start to pay closer attention. If I don't notice any feeling of sedation for a few days in a row, this typically means something is changing.

Even more concerning is when my medications don't have the same effect on me when I take them at night. Usually my antipsychotic medication makes me so drowsy that I fall asleep even if I am trying to stay awake, and I will sleep for at least six hours. If I notice that it is taking longer than normal for my medications to make me feel sleepy or if they don't make me feel tired at all, I contact my psychiatrist.

How frequently are my moods changing? I am a fairly emotional guy by nature. I am pretty sensitive to strong emotions in other people, but I pay attention if I notice I am getting overly emotional in a given week. Even when my medications are working well, my mood is constantly changing under the surface. I will have periods of depressive symptoms that are very minor but noticeable, even during periods of the year when I am normally very healthy. I will also have periods where my mood is a little higher than normal and I have more energy but not impairment. I pay very close attention to these fluctuations.

I also experience an in-between state where my mood is neither up nor down but in transition; this is usually accompanied by a nagging, unstable feeling. Because I've gotten accustomed to this volatility, unless my mood has gone too far up or down, I don't worry too much. If it takes a week or more for my mood to shift from one pole to the other, I don't worry, but if I notice that nagging feeling and resultant change in mood occurring more than once a week. I pay closer attention to my mood and other important areas of life. If this switch in mood happens in a one- to two-day period, I get concerned and if it happens in a single day I know that things are really bad. Rapid fluctuations in my mood are a very clear indicator that a manic episode is very close.

How am I doing in terms of mental bandwidth?
I pay close attention to my capacity to process information and manage stress. During times just preceding past manic episodes, I felt overwhelmed. My mind was overloaded and overstimulated, and when that went on too long, I would reach a point where I couldn't lighten the load, even when I was trying to reduce activities or stress. My thoughts accelerated and I felt driven to stay active mentally and physically. I began to have delusional, distressing thoughts, and at some point something snapped and mania began.

Because my job requires a lot of mental expenditure, I now track how much my mind can handle each day. When I have been under stress and very busy for a few weeks, sometimes I will begin to notice that it is hard to slow my mind down in the evening. Even the smallest stimuli feel like too much. When this happens, I take time off work and essentially attempt to think about nothing. I've learned to essentially put my mind to sleep for a few days. I don't spend time with anyone, I don't read anything, I don't leave the house, I don't use my phone or stare at any kind of screen, I don't spend much time in bright light (but I don't stay in the dark), I don't think about work or relationships other than my relationships with Bobbi and the kids. I try to completely ignore the outside world, but I am careful not to allow myself to retreat to internal thoughts where delusions can easily take root. I just meditate on God's Word, pray, and rest. Meditating and praying calm my mind and help to keep out what I am trying to avoid. If I do this for three or four days, I can usually bounce right back and return to my daily life without too much loss of productivity.

How is my thinking? If I'm working too quickly and making mistakes or if I'm working too slowly and having trouble thinking through simple problems, I take notice. I also pay attention to how much information I can keep in mind. When my mental health is worsening, I have trouble retaining information and often get distracted or lose my train of thought. When this is happening, I know that I have to slow down any activities that require attention to detail. At work, I slow down the pace of everything I do and when I feel particularly slow in thought. I do any tasks that are menial or require less intense focus. While I have regained a lot of cognitive ability, my working memory remains impaired, so I have to use checklists and reminders to stay on task.

I also pay attention to the clarity of my thoughts. I look for signs of problems in how I communicate verbally and what I write. If I notice emails or other work correspondence are missing words or are incoherent, or if people seem to have difficulty understanding me, it is a sign I need to slow down.

Obviously, a reliable indicator of worsening mental health is the appearance of paranoid or delusional thoughts. I occasionally struggle with intrusive, paranoid thoughts and can generally push them aside and refute them. They don't catch me off guard anymore, but I do take them very seriously. I have learned that if I work on the causes of what become delusions when I'm manic while I'm still healthy, then those things will be less of a problem when I get sick. As much as I hate looking back at my manic episodes, I have realized that I can learn from them, which helps me to think about handling them differently in the future. It is a way I can take control of an illness that feels out of control.

I pay attention to the general themes of my thoughts as a whole and take stock at the end of each day. I do most of my Bible reading and prayer in the evening and use this time to check my thoughts and orient them to the truth of God's Word. A helpful byproduct of all this monitoring is that it makes it more likely I will also notice my sin as it appears during the day. I am still vulnerable to being blind to sin but watching my mind has been a good safeguard for me.

How are my relationships? Every morning I ask myself how my attitude toward the Lord is. Do I have a heart turned to him in reverent love and obedience or are there things in my life that are interfering? I think about my current state and check for evidence of my pride or my recurring tendency to seek my own glory in life or my habit of depending on myself or other things instead of God. When I see those things, I repent and pray that God change me. I also assess my relationship with Bobbi and how my attitude is toward her. Then I check my attitude toward our children, my work, my boss and coworkers, my extended family, and my local church relationships. If I notice any problems in any of those areas, they become the focus of my prayers. When my heart is rightly turned toward God in reverence and love, then a proper attitude toward everyone else tends to flow from that.

STRATEGIES FOR MANAGING DEPRESSION

Over time, I have developed a few key steps to manage depression.

Keep up with important obligations to prevent additional stress. When I get depressed, it is easy to get behind at work and at home. I feel so tired and disconnected from others that I can become distant from Bobbi Jo and the kids. Feeling as if I am not loving my family well and falling behind at work generates a tremendous amount of stress. If I don't address it, I become overwhelmed and actually get further behind and more disconnected. If I let myself put things off, I may not get back to them for some time. Keeping up with all my responsibilities greatly reduces my stress level and helps keep guilty thoughts at bay. Whenever I find myself saying, "I don't feel like doing this or that," I force myself to do that very thing right then. This is a technique called behavioral activation. Being disciplined in this way is tiring but I know it will shorten the length of time I feel depressed. I don't notice any help in the moment but if I pay close attention, I start to notice that the combination of activity and stress begins to activate me. I have to do the exact opposite of this when I am concerned about becoming manic. In those times I have to reduce my activities and lower stress so that I can limit activation.

Activate myself and encourage good stress. I make a point to try and do more activities than I feel up to doing on a daily basis. I find this creates manageable, positive stress in my life, which contributes to getting better and out of an episode of depression more quickly.

Keep the focus on God and what he has done for me. It can be easy to retreat into my internal world when I get depressed. I can get overly self-focused, which brings out my innate selfishness. I try to ignore thoughts about how miserable I feel and instead list all the ways God has blessed me and how kind he has been to me. This helps me to keep a proper perspective and focused outside myself on positive things. It also is helpful to remember that God is in control and that he providentially cares for me.

Do enjoyable activities. I don't enjoy anything when I get depressed, so I don't want to do anything. I have to force myself to work out, read, talk with my wife, play with my kids, spend time with friends, etc. While I don't feel like doing those things, on some level my body and mind get enjoyment out of them even though I don't like them in that moment. Forcing myself to do things I usually enjoy can help me get better faster.

Remind myself that it will get better. When I have been depressed for a while, I get so entrenched in that state that I can no longer remember what normal feels like. I have to tell myself that I have always gotten better and this, too, will pass. I tell myself that I will feel good again and enjoy life.

Consider what lessons I might be learning. In

an effort to keep perspective during depression, I will think about what I might be learning from this current episode. I ask myself how it has caused me to grow and depend on God. Reframing the experience helps me think about depression in a new way.

Monitor negative thoughts and counter them. If I don't refute negative thoughts as soon as they arise, they spread like weeds and choke out healthy thoughts. Negative thinking makes everything worse. Research has shown that reframing your thoughts so they are less negative and more accurate helps to improve depression.

Maintain waking routines. Even though I feel tired all the time, I know that I have to keep my same sleep/wake cycle. I don't let myself stay in bed in the morning even though I desperately want to at times. Keeping my sleep cycle consistent helps me get better faster.

Pay attention to the demands of relationships, work, and other responsibilities. Sometimes I feel so impaired that social interactions are painfully awkward, and I avoid them until I feel a bit better. I need to especially evaluate my ability to do quality work at my job. If I don't feel like I am up to it, I will take off a few days to work harder at getting healthy.

Communicate with the people around me. I need to check in with Bobbi regularly on how depressed I am so she knows how much she can expect from me and can plan accordingly to care for me if needed.

If I diligently monitor my mood and take action to address any problems that arise, I am confident I can stay mostly well and keep severe illness at bay. Using these strategies I have managed to avoid a full manic episode for more than seven years and have had only one severe depression in that time after an attempt to change one of my medications.

My medications could stop working as they have in the past but if I am doing this daily monitoring I will notice changes before it is too late. Paying close attention to all these inner workings may seem like a burden, but this routine surveillance can become habit. That doesn't mean it's not exhausting at times, but reminders like the brightly colored, impulsively sought tattoos inside each of my wrists remind me that I need to take care of myself.

ANCHORING MYSELF IN CHRIST

And finally—and most importantly—I must remember daily who I am, to whom I belong, and what ultimately gives me value and worth. As I passed through my late twenties I still viewed myself as a Christian, but my growing identity as a mentally ill person began to cast an ever-increasing shadow over my life. In those years, I was failing as a husband and as an employee, had lost my intellectual and social abilities, and my identity as a mentally ill person threatened to consume my whole sense of self. I held on to Christ, but I had placed so much of my hope and identity into the things I had lost or was losing that I was consumed with thoughts like, "What value do I have in this life?"

After my last manic episode, God, in his goodness, reminded me that he was my only true hope and that I was losing sight of what mattered most. God was stripping me of everything I had placed my hope in. God was teaching me that putting my worth in anything other than my identity as a Christian would inevitably disappoint. God showed me in his word that my value is far greater than I could ever have imagined. My idea of God was too small, my view of my sin was too small, and so my view of God's grace was too small. The majestic God, who is sovereign over all things and perfect in his holiness, showed me mercy I did not deserve. I could never earn it, yet he gave it—but it was a costly grace. "But God proves His own love for us in that while we were still sinners, Christ die for us!" (Rom. 5:8).

God the Son humbled himself by becoming a man. Jesus lived a sinless life, but out of love he offered it as a sacrifice. He died and suffered the punishment my sin deserved freely out of his great love for me. He took on my guilt and gave me his righteousness as a gift. God didn't open my eyes to my sin and my need for his forgiveness through Christ because there was something special about me or because I deserved it in some way. He gave this gift simply because he chose to. The God of the universe died a humiliating death on the cross and bore my sin because he loved me, while I was still an unlovely sinner. Nothing in this world could ever make me more valuable.

How could I believe the lie that I am worthless or that no one loves me? How could I believe the lie that I am just a failure and nothing else? My success or failure as the world sees it is a dim shadow in light of the cross of Christ and the joy of my salvation. I am not "bipolar" or "crazy" or a great success or a great failure. I am a Christian. I belong to Christ, forever.

If you are a Christian who struggles with mental

illness, I urge you to remind yourself each and every day that your value and identity is in Christ. He suffered and died for you and you belong to him. Be set free by this knowledge. Free from placing your worth in your successes or failures, free from believing the lies of mental illness, free from internalizing the stigma that people place on the mentally ill. Free from comparing your life to lives of those who don't struggle with mental illness. You are free to live a life of thankful obedience to Christ knowing that you don't have to earn his approval. You can serve him freely in love as you are guided by his Spirit. That is true freedom.

If you are not a Christian, I urge you to consider this identity and life as a redeemed follower of Christ. All God asks is that we come as we are, with all our sins and failures, and repent, knowing we have nothing to offer him, and then place our faith and hope in Jesus's death and resurrection on our behalf. Christ takes our guilt and gives us his perfection. This act of love brings us into his kingdom, frees us from the darkness of this world, and ensures our place with Christ in eternity. "He has rescued us from the domain of darkness and transferred us into the kingdom of the Son He loves. We have redemption, the forgiveness of sins, in Him." (Col. 1:13-14).

God's Providence

Not only has God graciously given me salvation, he has also provided the means for managing my illness. I met my first psychiatrist, Dr. A, after a hypomanic episode that coincided with finishing graduate school. At the time I didn't know it was a hypomanic episode, but I recognized that I needed more help than my primary care doctor could provide, so I made an appointment to see a psychiatrist. I was expecting an older, soft-spoken, bearded gentleman to greet me in the waiting room. Instead a diminutive British woman called my name and asked me to follow her to her office.

I was not sure what to make of her; Dr. A acted different than any doctor I had seen before. She did a full intake but in a very conversational and even sometimes meandering sort of way. She was neither flippant nor serious; she was quirky. When we got near the end of the intake, she asked me what I wanted to do. Confused, I asked her what she meant. She went on to offer a number of possible next steps in treatment but left the decision of how to proceed up to me. I declined her recommendation to try a medication designed to stabilize mood and decided to wait and see how my health went. She didn't challenge me. Instead she asked me to come back in a few months to check in.

Remaining untreated was a very bad idea. Less than a year later I was back in her office, this time with Bobbi, and completely out of my mind. Dr. A was exactly the same as she had been in our first meeting. I would come to learn that every time I came to see her she would be the same—calm and cooperative, never overbearing or never overly grim or serious. Just like our first meeting she said, "We could try this medication and see how it goes... or there is this other one you could try. This one might work a bit better for you at this point." Her approach was very light-touch. From the beginning she always said "we" when talking about my treatment, making it clear that we were a team and she wouldn't make decisions without me. This made it easier for me to trust her. Even at my sickest moments she remained steady, reassuring me that we would get me well again.

By our second meeting I was very sick, so I started taking an antipsychotic and a mood stabilizer with plans to quickly ramp up to high doses of each to arrest the mania. Because I had delayed treatment so long, this episode went on for months. In one of my first follow-up visits, I told her how badly my stomach hurt from the medications. She said, "Well, that won't do," and put in an order for the brand name version of the medication, which, in the case of this particular medication, was known to have fewer gastrointestinal side effects. I am sure she could see how impatient and restless I was so she kept talking to me as she worked on placing the electronic pharmacy order. She said something at that point that I will never forget. Annoyed by what I assume were internal roadblocks meant to keep her from prescribing the more expensive version of the medication, she said, "Someone will be very unhappy about this, but I don't care, it is what you need." This was the first of a number of occasions where she stood up for and supported me. At times when I suggested trying a new medication that she wasn't in support of, rather than refusing she said, "I don't think it is a great idea, but you can try." When whatever I had suggested inevitably went poorly, rather than reasserting herself as the expert, she would humbly say, "Well, now you know."

There is another conversation I had with her that I will never forget. After being pretty much constantly sick for years I was once again in her office to get family medical leave paperwork signed to cover another extended absence from work. I was completely disheartened and beginning to think that I was actually no longer able to work. I asked if it was time we talked about me being disabled. Maintaining her calm demeanor, she muttered, "Rubbish, that's rubbish. I don't want to hear anymore talk about that. We will get you well and put back together, and we will get you back to work. Don't worry." I never again allowed myself to think about giving up and letting this illness defeat me.

The way Dr. A spoke to me, the mutuality of our

relationship, and the way we worked together allowed me to trust her when I most needed to. She rarely gave directives unless I was severely ill, but when she did, I listened. Early in the last manic episode I had, Bobbi and I were in Dr. A's office and I had just done something really dumb. She looked at me and said "Micah, here is what you are going to do. You will give your keys and wallet to Bobbi Jo. Do you have access to any other money than what you are giving her? If so, give that up too. You are not to leave the house unless someone goes with you. Are we clear about this?" These were essentially the things I had to agree to so I could stay out of the hospital and I complied. I knew I could trust her and I knew that when I was sick I should listen to what she told me to do.

When I learned Dr. A was retiring, I was stunned. I went out to my car and cried, called Bobbi Jo, and then cried some more. It was difficult to accept that she would no longer be there if I got sick. In some of our research studies focused on mental health recovery I had interviewed people with significant mental health struggles and they talked about how devastating it was when a trusted doctor moved away or retired. I never understood why it was so upsetting until then. The thought of not having her available if I became impaired was hard to take. I grieved this loss for months. She left me with many months of medication refills so I didn't even bother looking for a new psychiatrist.

Eventually my health plan started pressing me to get set up with a new doctor. I had always heard good things about a certain psychiatrist, but it was almost impossible to get on his panel. I was not sure what to do and I had been praying about it regularly. One morning, after dropping off the kids at school, I got a call that he had an opening. He has been my doctor for several years now and he's exceptional. I am very blessed to be under his care. He does all the things Dr. A did as far as collaborating with me and he has pushed me to make a few medication changes that have actually allowed me to improve my health and functioning even more. God has been so good to me in this and has blessed me by giving me two doctors who have taken good care of me.

God has also blessed me with effective medications to manage this illness. I have taken a lot of different medications over the years, and my current medications are taken to prevent mania primarily and to treat depression secondarily. I take an antipsychotic and a mood stabilizer. In the past I have discontinued several medications due to intolerable side effects. I have a love-hate relationship with them. I love that they keep my thoughts in order and keep my mood and sleep regular, but I hate the way they make me feel sometimes.

My treatment is not perfect, but we have found that it is working well for me. The most noticeable side effect I experience is feeling a bit sedated most days, particularly in the mornings and particularly when I am struggling with the fatigue that accompanies depressed mood. Side effects can be pretty miserable when one has to take medications at very high dosages for acute treatment, but my maintenance level dosages are pretty tolerable, and I've come to consider the sedation a small trade off to keep healthy.

I know that some people, in particular some Christians, have differing perspectives on the use of psychiatric medications, ranging from the view they are generally good and necessary to feeling that medications are actually wrong for Christians to take. I also know that there are people with mental illnesses similar to mine who do not wish to take medications for various reasons. I will not attempt to address or discuss these diverse views, but I will explain why I take psychiatric medications and why it would actually be wrong for me, personally, not to.

I am a Christian through God's grace in Christ Jesus. I seek to follow his will and not my own. His clear will for my life is that I become more like Jesus, preach the gospel, and make disciples. I am also to be a husband and father. God has gifted me with a family and given me the responsibility of leading them, pointing them to Christ, teaching them God's word, protecting and loving them gently. I am commanded to love my wife sacrificially as Christ loved the church. I was also created to work and be fruitful and in doing so provide for my family. All of this I am to do with a heart turned toward God in thankfulness and worship, acknowledging everything I have, including my life, is a gift from him.

In order to fulfill the roles God has given me I need every aid made available in God's providential care. The only authority on salvation and guide to living a life pleasing to God is found in his eternal Word. There is no higher authority. Scripture guides me in my role as servant of Christ, father, husband, worker, friend, and as a member of a local church. "All Scripture is inspired by God and is profitable for teaching, for rebuking, for correcting, for training in righteousness, so that the man of God may be complete, and equipped for every good work" (2 Tim 3:16-17).

God's Word can equip me for every good work in all my roles in life. But at the same time, "equipped for every good work" is not the same as able to do every good work a person is equipped and gifted to perform. One can be fully equipped in the word to do every good work but if he is hindered by physical infirmity, he is limited in what work he can actually do.

I use physical infirmity as an example because that is what I suffer from. The brain is an organ and it is the frailty of my brain that can take away my sanity. I have no doubt that something is wrong with my brain. What that is exactly and how it works itself out, I am not sure, but modern neuroscience seems to indicate that it is extremely complicated. Contention that what I suffer from is anything other than a biologically based illness that is beyond my control in many ways is just wrong.

I have spent the last fourteen years examining myself, observing this illness, and trying to understand what is happening all while doing research on mental illnesses for a living. In the last seven years I've had three episodes where I began getting manic, but what kept me out of the hospital were psychiatric medications. Only heavy doses of antipsychotics brought those burgeoning manic episodes to an end. If I chose not to take those medications, I would be unable to consistently, effectively, and faithfully raise and teach my children; serve, lead, and protect my wife; or work.

Without medication my children and wife would have to live with the constant rise and fall of my health, losing two to three months to a father likely in the hospital for his safety and theirs, then seven months of a lifeless father recovering from the ravages of mania, followed by nine months of a severely depressed father who struggled to do daily activities. Lest you think I am being dramatic, I am not. Without medication, my family and I face this fate.

God has given me His Spirit and His word. He has also given me a forgiving, intelligent, incredibly competent wife who also happens to be an exceptional clinical psychologist. He has given Bobbi and I jobs that provide us comprehensive insurance that allows me to see an excellent doctor who provides me with imperfect but effective psychiatric medications. All of these things are God's providential care in my life. These mercies enable me to do the work he has equipped and gifted me to do.

Wisdom tells me to be diligent in taking my medications, to be disciplined in caring for my mind and body and to earnestly and regularly practice the spiritual disciplines to grow in Christ and love for God. I believe that failure to do any of those three things would be foolishness on my part and a rejection of God's clear providential care for me. God has shown me that these medications allow me to use the gifts he has given me and to faithfully fulfill the responsibilities he has entrusted me with. Choosing to forgo them would be tantamount to choosing to fail in my duties as a husband, father, worker, church member, or friend. I understand why some people do not like to take these medications, but for me, they are a small price to pay for all that God allows me to do when I am using them.

I have not mentioned counseling in this book simply because, as an adult, I have never been to a therapist. I think counseling, with a well-trained psychologist or therapist, can be very beneficial in getting and staying well. I know many people who have benefited from therapy. Because of my introspective nature, I never felt that I needed assistance from a counselor. Paranoia and pride were also barriers at times. Bobbi is probably right in thinking that it could have been helpful during our difficult early years.

A Gift
from God

When I reflect on the twenty-five years that I have M struggled with bipolar disorder and the ways God has used it to make me more like Christ, to foster a greater dependence on him, and to deepen my love and devotion for my Savior, I am led to the certainty that this illness has actually been a God-given blessing. It was actually necessary for me to become more like Jesus.

The writer of Hebrews says we should pursue holiness because "without it no one will see the Lord" (Heb 12:14). The apostle Peter states, "But as the One who called you is holy, you also are to be holy in all

113

your conduct; for it is written, Be holy, because I am holy" (1 Pet 1:15). The work of being made holy began the day I was justified by my faith in Christ and sealed with his Spirit. God's word promises "that He who started a good work in you will carry it on to completion until the day of Christ Jesus" (Phil.1:6). God is in the process of perfecting me as his Son is perfect, and he will continue this work until I die or until Christ returns.

I have always been stubborn and rebellious. I am incredibly selfish by nature and do not listen well to instruction. I heard the gospel as a kid in church, but it meant nothing to me. God was an abstract idea and I was the center of my universe. I was told the news of the greatest gift I could ever receive, but I could not hear it and thus did not receive it nor pay it much notice. Even the death of my sister did not cause me to turn to God in faith. Even after God opened my eyes and ears to the truth of the gospel, my obstinate behavior remained. There is no way around it, I am a selfish, stubborn sinner. This pattern repeated itself over the first eight years of my marriage. Again, I had a tremendous gift sitting right in front of me, but I did not pay much notice.

What changes someone like me? Clearly, left to my own devices, I would continue on my way forever, selfish and immature. God in his goodness and wisdom, however, gave me an illness that broke me down, stripped me of my pride, dignity, mental abilities, relationships, social gifts, and repeatedly took away my sanity. Yet in all of it, the one consistent, real truth was God himself. After each mental illness episode I could see how everything had been chaotic, but God was unchanged. I had felt completely alone, cut off from everyone and everything, except God had been with me. He was always my anchor, he held me in the storm.

I was learning that if I loved God, I would obey him in everything. Jesus said in John 14:23-24, "If anyone loves Me, he will keep My word. My Father will love him, and We will come to him and make Our home with him. The one who doesn't love Me, will not keep My words."

I was a failure at keeping God's Word and I needed his help to mature into a man who would keep Jesus's commands and show himself to be a true disciple. God has mercifully helped me and he has done it through the loving discipline of a father.

Hebrews 12:4-11 says:

"In struggling against sin, you have not yet resisted to the point of shedding your blood. And you have forgotten the exhortation that addresses you as sons:

> My son, do not take the Lord's discipline lightly or faint when you are reproved by Him, for the Lord disciplines the one He loves and punishes every son He receives.

Endure suffering as discipline: God is dealing with you as sons. For what son is there that a father does not discipline? But if you are without discipline – which all receive – then you are illegitimate children and not sons. Furthermore, we had natural fathers discipline us, and we respected them. Shouldn't we submit even more to the Father of spirits and live? For they disciplined us for a short time based on what seemed good to them, but He does it for our benefit, so that we can share His holiness. No discipline seems enjoyable at the time, but painful. Later on, however, it yields the fruit of peace and righteousness to those who have been trained by it."

God has used this illness to discipline me to yield good fruit for his glory. I could not be the man that I am today, imperfect as I still am, had God not given me this illness. I can clearly see how time and again he used this illness to grow me spiritually and change me into a different person. Far from being a sign that I am somehow cursed by God, this illness and the fruit born out of it are actually evidence that I am blessed by him.

I have come to understand through all of this that ultimately, it is God who gave me this mind and he is sovereign over my sanity. I have been pretty healthy and stable for more than seven years through discipline, good medication management, and hard work, but I believe God has given me all of those things. He taught me to be disciplined and to work hard. The medications are his good gift of providence, but ultimately my health rests in God's hands. If I am well, he is in control. If I am sick, he is in control. Either way, he is always good. His goodness does not depend on my circumstances. If my medications should stop working for me, is not God's hand in that? God's hand is in the present state of stability I am blessed to enjoy. If he should remove that stability, do I have any right to complain? If he does so, then I believe it will be for my own good, however painful and difficult that may be.

I never want to lose my sanity again, but good health and a sane mind are not promised to me— sanctification and glorification through Christ are (Rom 8:30; Heb 10:10). I know he will continually make me more like his Son through the sanctifying work of the Holy Spirit, but what that will look like in future is unknown to me. This illness may continue in its present state, it may get better, or it may get worse, but God and his promises will remain unchanged.

You or a loved one may have struggled with mental illness, and it may be difficult for you to see how that illness could ever be a blessing. I speak only for myself in light of the great change that God has wrought in me. While I see this illness as a blessing, I confess that it has been a miserable one. Numerous times I have thought that I have reached the end of what I can endure, and I desperately have called out to God to take it away. As the illness always went on, I found myself grasping hold of Christ and praying with my whole heart. At that point, at the end of myself, he has often delivered me from my suffering. I can't speed up that process. It isn't until he makes me truly desperate that my cry for mercy is made with all that I am.

The fact that I could recover and once again experience sanity with a different and greater strength taught me that it was God who sustained and healed me. He allows us to become completely spent so that we will find our all in him. If we are willing to learn from his providential sanctification, we will come away with a clearer picture of who God is and we will have gained an even higher view of our creator. When I endure my illness, I know that I will learn from it. God will reveal more of himself to me if I will view it through the truth of his Word and earnestly seek him in prayer.

God's plan is to make us holy, not bless us with earthly health or material blessing. It is often our good health or possessions that hinder us in becoming more like Christ. Should we seek out hardship or poverty to be more godly? Absolutely not. But we should be aware that what the Bible calls blessings from God are not what the world considers blessings. I desperately need God and the life he gives through his Son's death and resurrection. This is true in all circumstances, whether I am sick or well. I only have one true and eternal hope, and that is Christ.

A Restored Life and Marriage

If you've skipped ahead to the end, we don't blame you. In many ways we wish we could have skipped ahead, too, or at least been reassured that we would make it to the point where we find ourselves today. When Micah first apologized to me for the ways in which he had let us down, I was skeptical that things would change. I am so glad to say I was wrong.

The difference in his affection, attitude, and engagement with our family, his helpfulness, and his patience was apparent immediately. As his health steadily improved and he maintained these changes, I began to believe that he might actually be a new man, until one day

I had a realization that filled me with guilt. For a long time I had attributed Micah's failings and limitations to his character and stubborn unwillingness to change. Disappointments in our early marriage powerfully shaped the way I thought about him for the next several years. We had enjoyed very little healthy time together after we were married. Now I was faced with an almost completely different person. Here now was someone who reminded me of that younger man I had fallen in love with, someone who was attentive and sensitive, who could see outside himself again and notice people who were hurting and do something about it, someone who laughed easily and made others feel like everything was going to be okay. I felt guilty because I realized that he had been there all along, but now he was finally free from the burdens of illness. I had to apologize for misjudging him.

Seven years ago we both thought that we would continue to struggle as we had and that we would just have to suffer, which we were committed to doing. Now, it's almost unbelievable how good things have become, how in love we are with each other, how much fun we have together, and even how well we manage the conflicts that arise in every marriage. We both understand that we can't take credit for what we have—it is a gift God has given. He was the one who changed us, he was the one who restored our marriage, and we trust that he will be the one who sustains us going forward. We have only to be faithful to follow God's command for husbands and wives to love each other sacrificially. We acknowledge that our efforts will only succeed by the power of his Spirit working in us.

Addressing Suicide

Suicide. It's a topic that has brought me the most sadness in the seventeen years that I have been doing research with people who live with mental illnesses. Part of my job is to assess the risk of suicide among people in our research studies who indicate, either in an interview or on a questionnaire, that they have been thinking about ending their lives. Unfortunately, I've had a lot of experience with these risk evaluations. I would like to address anyone reading this book who might be thinking about taking his or her own life or who has thought about it in the past and still considers it an option.

M

First, to my fellow Christian, you may have entertained any number of justifications for taking your own life. Maybe you have convinced yourself that you are a burden to your family or friends and that they would be better off without you. Sure, your death will cause them pain, but you tell yourself they will get over it. Maybe you've stopped thinking about family and friends all together.

It could be that you have no one in your life, so you reason that it won't matter if you are gone. Maybe you have convinced yourself that taking your own life is fine, on some level, because God will forgive you, or that by dying you can be with him sooner. Or maybe you have stopped caring about any justification other than your desire to escape the misery of unbearable and unrelenting suffering. I can relate to feeling so distraught.

All of the aforementioned thoughts have passed through my mind at one time or another and I have had to wrestle with them. In every case the one thing that always remained an obstacle was God. I wondered how I would justify my suicide to God. While I would reassure myself that God is forgiving and Christ's death is sufficient to cover all my sins, it still bothered me that I would be presuming upon God's grace to commit a grievous sin, which suicide most certainly is, in the hopes that he would forgive me. To do so would be acting, in a sense, as if God owed me forgiveness and because of that I could act as I wished, expecting that he would grant me the forgiveness I deserved. But therein lies the problem: I *don't* deserve anything from him. God did not forgive me based on any merit on my part. He loved me and his son died a substitutionary death on my behalf while I was still in rebellion against him. How could I then plan to commit a serious sin, expect his forgiveness, and consider myself regenerate with a heart turned toward God in reverent love?

God revealed to me that I had been thinking about this incorrectly from the very start because I was starting with me. I was the reference point from which I framed this struggle. It was *my* desire to escape my loneliness, *my* pain, *my* suffering, and most foolishly it was *my* life. Except it is not my life. It does not belong to me. God gives the very breath I take, moment to moment. None of the loneliness, pain, or suffering, nor any of the justifications for escaping them, have any bearing on taking my own life, simply because it is not my life to take.

It is not your life to take. Your life belongs to our God and Creator. He is the proper reference point. He is the place where we must begin when struggling with this temptation. When I began to frame my thinking in this way, starting with God and Christ's work on the cross and confessing that this life does not belong to me, the temptation of suicide lost its power over me.

You might be thinking that this is easy for me to say and that I don't know your struggle. You are right—I do not know what it is like for you. I can't understand how alone you feel or what it is like for you to suffer with your particular mental illness. You're the only person who knows that. What I can say is that I have felt completely alone. I have spent significant periods of time so severely depressed for so long that I feared I would never get better. I have struggled with people thinking I am lazy and just don't try hard enough to get better. I have felt embarrassed by my inability to do simple, everyday activities and engage in simple, everyday social interactions. I have watched life pass by while I faltered and stumbled through it. I have felt my sanity slipping away, over and over, and then lived for months without it. When it returned, each time it was as if I had lost more of myself. I have felt ashamed of the crazy things I said and did while I was manic; I have spent significant periods of time immersed in my memories.

I have sobbed and pleaded with God to please take this away: "Please return my sanity, if not for me than for my family. Let me suffer in other ways, but be merciful and return my sanity. Please end this suffering. Please lift your hand. Relent; I can't bear this anymore. It is too much. Why do you allow this to go on so long? Will it ever end? Please be merciful. What am I supposed to be learning? How can I ever work for your kingdom in this state? If this continues there will be nothing left of me."

I may not understand your struggle, but God does, and what he endured on the cross dwarfs any suffering you or I may have in this life. Jesus was fully God, but he was also fully a human, like you and I, and he bore the full justice of God's wrath for every single person he set apart as objects of undeserved mercy. I cannot even fathom the depths of that suffering. Only he can know such suffering, and he is the one who loves us and has adopted us into his family as sons and daughters. Jesus Christ is our great treasure, and our prize is eternity with him. We get to enjoy him forever. The path marked out toward that prize lies in obedient love to him.

Taking a life that is not your own is the wrong path. He is the good shepherd who gathers his sheep, but don't delude yourself into thinking that suicide is an acceptable way to be with Christ sooner or that your motivation in some way is to be with him. The desire to be with him should be grounded in love, and we show that love by obeying his commands and loving others. Finish the race well as a good and faithful servant. He suffered far more than we can imagine, and he endured until the end. We must also endure until the end. There is hope, and Christ alone is that eternal, unchanging hope.

If you are not a Christian, I urge you to consider the hope that is Jesus Christ and the gift of grace, eternal life, and the indwelling of the Holy Spirit that only he can offer. Know that you are created in the image of God, which means that your life and the life of every other human being has tremendous value. Trust that the One who created you and breathed life into you is able to pour into you a new life—not the empty, dying life of this world but an eternal life where joy and love for God is ever growing for eternity. God has given me this new life through his Son and salvation is a special joy that permeates every part of me. It's a joy that I can appreciate even when I can appreciate and feel nothing else. I pray that you will know this joy and rest in the hope that is found in Jesus Christ.

Do not give up. I cannot promise that your illness will get better anytime soon, nor can I guarantee that the impairments your illness causes will improve. I can promise that if you place the point of reference for how you think about yourself in Christ and his redemptive work on the cross, and also pursue and receive adequate mental health treatment, things will eventually get better. It will take time, but it is possible.

I leave you with the words of Paul in Philippians 4:8:

> "Finally brothers, whatever is true, whatever is honorable, whatever is just, whatever is pure, whatever is lovely, whatever is commendable – if there is any moral excellence and if there is any praise – dwell on these things."

Nothing is more commendable, honorable, just, lovely, praiseworthy, or pure than the love of God displayed at the cross where his perfect mercy and perfect justice meet in the sacrificial death of Jesus Christ. Dwell on this awesome truth and "be transformed by the renewing of your mind" (Rom. 12:2).

Bibliography

American Psychiatric Association. (2013). *Diagnostic and statistical manual of mental disorders, Fifth edition (DSM-5)* (Vol. First). Washington DC: American Psychiatric Association.

Made in the USA
Coppell, TX
30 June 2020